POLICE WRITING

THIRD EDITION

KAREN JAKOB

National Library of Canada Cataloguing in Publication

Jakob, Karen, 1953-
A guide to police writing/Karen Jakob. — 3rd ed.

First ed. published under title: The complete guide to police writing.
Includes index.
ISBN 0-459-27327-2

1. Police reports. 2. Report writing. 3. English language — Rhetoric. I. Title.

HV7936.R53J34 2002 808'.066363 C2002-903944-4

Printed in Canada

One Corporate Plaza
2075 Kennedy Road
Toronto, Ontario
M1T 3V4

Customer Relations
Toronto 1-416-609-3800
Elsewhere in Canada/U.S. 1-800-387-5164
Fax 1-416-298-5094
World Wide Web: http://www.carswell.com
E-mail: orders@carswell.com

To John and Lisa
with love

Preface

Police officers and law enforcement students need to fight the paperwork — and win. The battle against crime is not just fought in the streets. It is often the quality of the paperwork that decides which side wins. Strong writing skills are critical elements at every stage of the investigation and prosecution.

The ability to communicate effectively is the key to the future of policing. Understanding that written communication is essentially a one-way process is also significant to the law enforcement professional. There are no opportunities for the reader to question what is meant or clarify information directly. While modern dictation processes have relieved many police officers of their need for penmanship or keyboarding skills, the need for clarity and precision has increased. Without such clarity and precision the entire communication process grinds to a halt until the reader has the chance to truly understand what has been written. Good writing skills make good communication possible.

This book is designed to help police officers and law enforcement students to develop good writing skills. It provides a practical, rather than a theoretical, approach to writing. It serves as an "Owner's Manual" for language so that problems can be solved quickly. By recognizing the requirements of good police writing and by understanding how the fundamental rules of the language work, officers can improve the quality of their writing quickly and easily. Good paperwork strengthens the judicial system and improves the officer's professional image.

The first part of this book deals with on-the-job police writing. Reports, notebooks, and memos are the most common forms of writing for police officers. The police writing part emphasizes the importance of documents and the need to develop the skills to write these documents clearly. While the specific format for police writing varies from one jurisdiction to another, the fundamental principles of precise and effective writing remain the same. As a result, the focus of the first part of the book is on how to write well rather than on specific details of forms.

The second part of this book examines the rules and conventions of the English language. It serves as a reference manual for police officers to ensure that what they write is correct. Grammatical terms have been kept to a minimum, and explanations are supported by examples that are relevant to police writing.

The final part of the book discusses the process of writing essays and research papers. Officers who are on training courses or who take post-secondary courses are often required to write essays or research papers. Some departments also use essays as part of the assessment process for promotions. This section explains the process of writing a good paper and includes guidelines for documenting source material, so that plagiarism problems are avoided.

Finally, an Appendix is included to provide examples of commonly used police report forms.

A Guide to Police Writing can be used as a reference text to solve on-the-job writing problems. It can also be a resource for classroom use in college courses or for in-service training courses.

TO THE READERS

If you have any suggestions or comments about this book, or if you would like more information about police writing, please contact me directly by writing to:

Karen Jakob
P.O. Box 506
Acton, Ontario
Canada, L7J 2M8

Acknowledgments for the Third Edition

Books do not grow in isolation. This revised edition is based on comments and suggestions I received concerning the first and second editions. After the first edition was published, I continued to lecture at police colleges and academies. This experience strengthened my understanding of the requirements of police writing. I conducted more research in the field and met many people who have kindly shared information with me. As my experience increases, my belief in the need for good police writing also increases. Obviously, this belief is shared by many members of the police community.

I would like to thank all of the students who attended my classes at the FBI National Academy in Quantico, Virginia; the Southwestern Law Enforcement Institute in Dallas, Texas; and the Ontario Police College in Aylmer, Ontario. These students helped me to develop an approach to police writing that is both realistic and practical.

Special thanks are extended to the FBI Academy, particularly the 163rd and 164th sessions of the National Academy, the Education and Communications Arts Unit, the Behavioral Sciences Unit, and the National Center for the Analysis of Violent Crime. These students and friends helped me to refine my writing and survive the editing process. I am especially grateful to the Southwestern Law Enforcement Institute for its continuing support and encouragement.

Special thanks goes to Michael Wood for his hard work on the third edition. Without his help, this edition would not be as relevant and current. Thanks also goes to Inspector Robert Dymock, St. Thomas Police Service, Ontario, for providing the sample police report forms.

Thanks also goes to Bernie Aron, Jilean Bell, and Jennifer Hashimoto for all of their hard work and patience.

I would also like to thank my friends Robert Legault, Sheila Attwell, Lorne Moore, Dave and Pat Astley, Bob and Judy Woolsey, Peter and Ann Waldon, Ro and Bill Waldon, Mary Ellen Wagner, Judy Riepma, Belle, and the GORGG gang.

Acknowledgments for the Second Edition

I would like to thank the following individuals for their contributions and their support of my work:

Edward Tully, Unit Chief, Education and Communications Arts Unit, FBI Academy
Margo Bennett, Bob Bonshire, Tom Christenberry, Les Davis, Ginny Field, John Hess, Larry Levine, Nick Londino, John Mulvihill, Leon Schenck, Sharon Smith, Ancil Sparks, and Karen Zink of the Education and Communications Arts Unit, FBI Academy, 1990
Stephen Amico, Secret Service, National Center for the Analysis of Violent Crime
Owen Einspahr, FBI, New York City Regional Training Co-ordinator
Dr. Gary Sykes, Director, Southwestern Law Enforcement Institute
Dan Carlson, Southwestern Law Enforcement Institute
Steve Metelsky, Manager, Policing Services Division, Ontario Police Commission
Larry Godfree, Director, Ontario Police College
Martin van Weert, Deputy Director, Ontario Police College
Bob Brock, Chief Instructor, Ontario Police College
Michael ("Maxie") Wood, Chief Instructor, Ontario Police College
Bill Tavener, Instructor, Ontario Police College
Allen Montgomery, Instructor, Ontario Police College
Chuck Lawrence, Instructor, Ontario Police College
Staff Sergeant Glenn MacPhail, Canadian Police College

Sergeant Ron Lewis, Canadian Police College
Inspector Dan Reid, Halton Regional Police
Detective John Sinclair, Metropolitan Toronto Police
Detective Superintendent Kate Lines, Ontario Provincial Police
Senior Sergeant Bronwyn Killmier, South Australia Police Department
Sergeant Lorne Moore, Hamilton-Wentworth Regional Police
Sergeant Rick Bodnar, Niagara Regional Police
Sergeant John McKay, Nepean Police
Constable Brian Carter, Peel Regional Police
James MacDonald, Chairman, Human Studies Division, Humber College of Applied Arts and Technology
Wayson Choy, Professor of English, Humber College
Dr. Greig Henderson, Professor, English Department, University of Toronto
Sheila Attwell, VIP Services Co-ordinator, University of Guelph
Eric Elstone, freelance writer

I would also like to acknowledge the contribution of the late George Evans, former co-ordinator of the Law and Security Administration programme at Humber College. I would also like to fondly remember the contributions of the late Professor Earl Reidy and the late Professor Jacques Picard of Humber College. Their friendship, inspiration, and courage will not be forgotten.

Finally, the biggest thanks go to my husband, John, for being my best editor, and to my daughter, Lisa, for being my best fan.

Table of Contents

Part Two
A Reference Guide for Better Writing Skills

Part Three
Essays and Research Papers

PART ONE
POLICE WRITING

1

Police Reports

It is essential to assume that every report is a "public" document which will reflect the professionalism of you and your department. Unfortunately, while reports may be written under less than ideal conditions, they may be read by critical readers who have the luxury of reviewing the reports at their leisure. The police report is not an "in-house" document. It may be read by other government agencies, insurance companies, lawyers, judges, or jurors. Freedom of Information legislation allows the media and the public greater access to previously "classified" documents, including police reports.

The significance of each report should not be minimized. A poorly written report may give the impression that the investigation itself was sloppy and that your organizational skills are weak. This could weaken your image at promotion time and damage your credibility when you take the stand in court.

All of the hard work done during an investigation could be wasted if a criminal cannot be brought to trial and convicted on the basis of the information in the police report. Before you decide to "get the paperwork out of the way as quickly as possible," consider the significance of the document you are preparing.

Unfortunately, the judicial system does not move quickly. However, a good report can withstand this time delay. If the report is well written at the time of the occurrence, it will still be well written when the case comes to trial. On the other hand, a report that is "dashed off" may return to haunt you later as you scramble to explain errors or to supply missing information. The initial report is the basis for all of the subsequent documents and investigation related to the case. An inadequate report undermines all subsequent documents based on it, such as Crown briefs, bail hearing sheets, or search warrants. Follow-up investigation depends on the original report containing all of the necessary information.

As the extent of computerization increases, the importance of the initial report also increases. For example, sections of the police report may be transferred directly through a computer to the Crown brief or to other court-related documents. While this saves typing time, it also means that any errors in the original will be reproduced every time the original is moved from one document to another.

Information from reports may also be the basis for computer databases. The computer database, drawn from the reports, makes the cross-referencing of information easy if correct and complete information is provided in the original reports. For this reason, more demands are being made on report writers to provide accurate and complete information for occurrences which may, at the time, appear to be minor. For example, the information from a simple "barking dog" complaint may provide information critical to a more serious investigation. For example, that barking dog complaint may signal the exact time of a break and enter which another officer is investigating in the same neighbourhood. As well, the statistics from the report may be used for crime pattern identification and may provide records for Statistics Canada.

The report serves as a record of events and actions. It provides the facts of a case and forms the basis of follow-up activities. Even if a case does not result in a charge and conviction, the reports keep fellow officers informed and help to avoid unnecessary duplication of work.

1. GENERAL OCCURRENCE REPORTS

Every police service has forms for general occurrence reports. These reports are used for occurrences such as arrests, stolen or seized vehicles, fraudulent documents, missing persons, homicides or sudden deaths, and other general occurrences. While the exact format of these reports may vary from one service to another, the forms are similar in design.

Well-designed forms can help you to include all of the required information since they standardize the placement of the information so that anyone who is familiar with the form can find specific entries quickly. Generally, the forms have two sections: the "fill in the blanks" section and the narrative section.

(a) The "Fill in the Blanks" Section

This section of the report *appears* to be the easiest to complete. The heading in each blank gives guidelines for the type of information required in that space. However, the guidelines are only effective if the writer understands what information is required and gives accurate information. The pitfall of the blank space is that the writer gives information which fits the space rather than information which is complete.

When completing the "fill in the blanks" section, you may find it difficult to describe all of the details in the space provided. If more space is needed, insert the phrase "see narrative" or "see below", instead of trying to find a one- or two-word phrase to describe every detail or action.

Another problem with this section is the fact that you may not have the information needed for each blank box. It is always better to put something in the space to tell the reader that you have looked at the question and have considered a response. If information is unknown, say so. The reader needs to know that the information is unavailable. If you do not explain this, the reader may decide, mistakenly, that you simply forgot to include the information.

Information in the report is more likely to be correct if you develop a consistent system for recording information in your notebook and then transferring that information to the report form. For example, filling in each blank space in the order in which it appears on the form is better than jumping around from blank space to blank space. If you are familiar with the order in which the information is required to appear on the form, it is easier to remember what information must be gathered during the investigation itself.

Finally, it may be acceptable to use short forms for the "fill in the blanks" section of the report. Just make sure that you are using abbreviations approved by your department, rather than abbreviations of your own creation. Common abbreviations include LKA for "last known address" or N/A for "not applicable".

(b) The Narrative Section

The narrative section of the report describes what happened. Remember that the reader of the report is relying on you to give a clear description of events. There are two areas to be concerned about when writing the narrative: the information, and the way the information is presented.

After the investigation is finished, review the information you have collected. It is very important to be able to distinguish between information in your notes that is relevant to the report and information that is irrelevant. In order to include complete information in the report, ask yourself "When, Where, Who, What, Why, and How" questions. If you ask yourself these questions in this order, you will find that the information is easily organized in the report.

1. When

When did this occurrence happen?
When did you arrive?
When did you speak to the victim and witnesses?
When did you leave?

2. Where

Where did the occurrence happen?
Where did you go?
Where is the victim?
Where is the property?
Where do the people involved live and work?
Where can people be contacted?

3. Who

Who is the victim?
Who is the complainant?
Who is involved?

Who are the witnesses?
Who is the suspect?
Who is the culprit?

4. What

What crime was committed?
What happened?
What did you do?
What was said?
What did the witnesses see?
What did the victim do?
What did the complainant report?

5. How

How did the crime happen?
How did the witnesses get involved?
How did you do your investigation?
How did you form your opinions?

6. Why

Why did the occurrence happen?
Why did you reach these conclusions?

Once you have a clear understanding of the information needed in the report, you can concentrate on the problem of writing that information so that the reader will understand it easily. The narrative must be

(i) factual
(ii) well organized
(iii) complete
(iv) concise
(v) correct
(vi) readable.

(*i*) *Factual*

It is essential that you follow your department's policy regarding the separation of facts, opinions, and conclusions. This is of great importance now that reports are accessible to the public through the Freedom of Information legislation.

Facts can be verified. Facts are the things that you know. For example, you could report that the victim had a six-inch gash on his right arm. You do not know how the gash got there, but you can verify that the gash *is* there.

Opinions may be included if they add information to the report, and if they are clearly identified as opinions and not facts. Opinions are based on what appears to be true or on an informed "gut reaction." These opinions are important to the investigation and help the investigator doing the follow-up work. However, opinions must not be confused with facts. For example, in your report, you may include the following statement: "This officer has the opinion that the gash was self-inflicted." However, if you are going to include an opinion, you must also include a description of the facts that support the opinion. For example, "This officer is of the opinion that the gash was self-inflicted. There was no one around and the victim was holding the knife in his left hand when police arrived. In addition, the victim is left-handed and was described as 'depressed' by a witness."

Opinions that express approval or disapproval should never be included in reports. For example, offering the opinion that "The accused was poorly dressed and looked like the type of crazy person who just wanted to get attention in this stupid way" is loaded with judgmental language which is unprofessional.

Conclusions are similar to opinions but should be based more solidly on fact. For example, while an opinion that a wound was self-inflicted might be supported by the fact that the victim was found holding the knife, a conclusion would be supported by more solid factual evidence such as fingerprints and eye-witness accounts of the stabbing. Conclusions are the deductions which can be drawn logically from the facts and opinions available. Again, conclusions should be clearly identified as such and not presented as fact. If the victim has a gash on his arm and the accused is standing beside the victim with a bloody knife in his hand, you could conclude that the accused stabbed the victim. However, this is a conclusion and not a fact. At this point, you cannot be sure that the accused stabbed the victim. Perhaps the accused only picked up the knife after it was dropped by someone else. To describe your conclusion, you could write "Based on the witnesses' descriptions of the fight and the evidence gathered at the scene, including the fingerprints of the accused found on the knife, the writer concluded that the victim was stabbed by the accused."

(*ii*) *Well Organized*

When information is well organized, the sequence of events is easy to follow. In order to organize the narrative of a general occurrence report, use an outline. This may seem like an extra step, but it will save you time in the long run. Since the narrative must be arranged in chronological order to describe events in a logical sequence from beginning to end according to time, make a time chart in your notebook. For example,

8:01 — Call Received
8:02 — Dispatched
8:05 — Arrived at scene
8:06 — Spoke to victim
Observed cut, knife, and blood
Applied towel to cut
8:08 — Ambulance called
Spoke to witnesses
8:15 — Ambulance arrives
8:21 — Ambulance leaves
8:23 — Additional witnesses interviewed
8:35 — 10-8

Notice that the outline does not contain all of the details that will be drawn from the notes and included in the report. The outline merely arranges events in chronological order so you can see the sequence in which everything happened before you begin to write your narrative.

Good planning will result in a well organized report. Few officers can take notes, interview witnesses, render first aid, and write the report simultaneously. Take both the investigation and the report one step at a time.

(*iii*) *Complete*

A complete account of the events, from beginning to end, leaves no questions in the reader's mind and no chance for misinterpretation. Problems are created when the information in reports is incomplete. For example,

The writer found a large knife and saw the victim bleeding. An ambulance was called and the victim was transported to hospital. The writer seized the knife as evidence.

This narrative leaves many questions unanswered, such as

Where was the knife found?
How badly was the victim bleeding?
Where were the injuries?
What ambulance was called?
Where was the victim treated for the injuries?
Where is the knife now?
Who witnessed the incident?
Why was the crime committed?
What investigation was done?

If you submit an incomplete report similar to the above example, it is likely your supervisor will return it to you to be rewritten. This will cost you (and your department) more time. If you must rewrite the report and did not get the necessary information at the scene, or do not have good notes for reference, you will lose even more time as you reinvestigate the call. In addition, if another officer is assigned to get the information for you or to do follow-up work based on the incomplete original report, you will not score any points with your colleagues or supervisors.

(iv) Concise

It may sound contradictory to say that reports must be complete and concise, but it is not. A complete report gives all of the necessary information. A concise report leaves out information that is not needed or not relevant.

One of the most important responsibilities of the report writer is to select the right information for the report. For example, it may be necessary to explain how you became involved and arrived at the scene. Were you dispatched, were you waved over by a witness, or were you driving by? However, there are some details that do not need to be included. For example,

> Officer Greenburg pulled into the driveway, blew his nose, got out of the car, straightened his tie, put on his hat and walked down the sidewalk. The sidewalk was lined with flowers which the officer admired for a moment, while reflecting on the fleeting beauty of nature, before arriving at the door. Officer Greenburg knocked on the door twice, in rapid succession, and while he waited he shone his shoes on the back of his pants.

Another cause of unnecessarily long reports is poor word choice. Use fewer words by choosing the best words. Phrases such as "at this point in time" could be shortened to "now" or "then" (depending on the structure of the sentence). Descriptions such as "without restricting the generality of the foregoing and subject to the exigencies of the force" could be deleted. These types of phrases are "filler" which add bulk without adding information.

(*v*) *Correct*

The information in the report must be accurate. For example, if there is an error in a person's birth date, that person could be listed incorrectly on a computer database and, later, confused with another person who has the same name. The omission of "east" or "west" from the street address on a search warrant could lead officers to the wrong address.

Simple spelling errors can also make the report, and the investigation itself, appear sloppy. For example, imagine the lawyer saying,

> "Your Honour, this officer has written that the victim was a Mr. Cowan. Now he states that Mr. Cohen suffered the injuries. How many other 'little inaccuracies' are contained in this report? How careless is this officer in his investigation if he cannot get a simple thing like the victim's name spelled correctly? Officer, do you have problems recording information accurately?"

In order to write properly, you must use words precisely. Imprecise wording annoys the reader and undermines the credibility of the report. For example, the sentence "The suspect consumed the parcel in his jacket" is confusing. Did the writer mean to use the word "concealed"?

Is this the description of someone who was hiding something in his coat? Is it merely the description of someone's peculiar eating habits?

Usage errors involve incorrect word choice. A common example of this type of error in police reports is the misuse of "premise" as the singular form of "premises". A premise is an idea which is proven in an argument, not a place. The word "premises" refers to a place.

Punctuation errors also cause problems. For example, there is a difference in the way these sentences are read depending on the punctuation used:

> The department will pay for repairs to the cars, sirens, and mufflers.
>
> or
>
> The department will pay for repairs to the cars' sirens and mufflers.

(*vi*) *Readable*

The police report has to be written so that it can be read and understood quickly. In order to do this, you must be able to take information from the investigation and put it into clear sentences. This is easier to do if you use an outline rather than try to find the information and write the report at the same time.

When the outline is transferred to the narrative, it must be coherent. Coherence is achieved by giving information in correct order and by using transitional words and phrases. For example, using the outline from point (ii) "Well Organized", above, the final report could read:

> At 08:01 hours on Tuesday the 25th of June 2002, the writer was dispatched to a disturbance call at 925 Harold Street, Binkham. At 08:05 hours, the writer arrived and spoke with Carl SWINDEN, the victim of this occurrence, who had a 30-centimetre laceration on the inside of the right forearm from the elbow to the wrist.
>
> SWINDEN indicated that an unknown assailant had attacked him approximately 20 minutes prior to the writer's arrival.
>
> The writer saw a large butcher knife sitting on the front step of the house with traces of blood on the blade. The knife was seized by the writer and was sealed in a plastic bag for identifi-

cation purposes. A large pool of blood by the front step led to the sidewalk in front of the house where the writer met the victim.

At 08:08 hours Binkham Memorial Ambulance was called to the scene by the writer, as SWINDEN appeared to be suffering from loss of blood. His voice was becoming weak and his speech incoherent.

While waiting for the ambulance to arrive, the writer spoke to George MONTY (927 Harold St., Binkham, phone 555-1212), who advised that SWINDEN has been acting strangely for the past two days. Further information from MONTY leaves the writer with the opinion that SWINDEN's wife has separated from him recently. This information cannot be confirmed to date.

At 08:15 hours, the ambulance arrived and transported SWINDEN to Memorial Hospital at 08:21 hours.

After securing SWINDEN's residence, the writer checked with the neighbours at 923 Harold St. for additional information as to a suspect. No information was obtained, and the residents were unaware of any problem with SWINDEN until contacted by the writer.

At 08:35 hours, the writer left the scene and attended at Memorial Hospital. The writer spoke with Dr. Margaret PATCHEM (501 Holyhock Ave., Moorefield, bus. ph. 555-1115, res. 555-3946), who said that SWINDEN passed out after arriving and would be unavailable for further questioning until tomorrow morning. There were no indications of the injury being life-threatening.

The writer also spoke with the emergency ward clerk, Ms. Karen DOODLE (413 Pineapple Place, Binkham, ph. 555-8994), who said that SWINDEN had signed in with his left hand. Examination of the signature appears to indicate that SWINDEN is naturally left-handed.

From the information available, the writer is of the opinion that the wound was self-inflicted. This opinion is shared by Dr. PATCHEM, who advised that the wound is consistent with a self-inflicted wound.

Further investigation will be done on June 26th by the writer. No further action will be required from this department unless it is requested by hospital staff.

It is easier for the reader to find important information in the report if it is highlighted visually. An example of visual highlighting is the custom of putting names in capitals in the report. Paragraphs can also highlight information by grouping similar events into logical units.

Also, remember that writing which is not legible is useless to the reader. If the information is important enough to put into the report, make sure it can be read and understood.

The need to be factual, well organized, complete, concise, correct, and readable when writing reports cannot be emphasized enough. While the importance of these factors is obvious on a general occurrence report, they are critical on a report where you are required to account for your actions. Submitting a "Use of Force" report that is not complete or correct can call your actions into question, affect your credibility or, in a worst-case scenario, cost you your job or result in you being convicted of an offence.

2. WRITING DESCRIPTIONS

Descriptions form the backbone of reports. Without complete and accurate descriptions, the reader cannot get a complete picture of people, events, or objects. It is frustrating for the reader to be faced with descriptions that are vague and general. Good descriptions provide specific details and aid investigations.

(a) Describing People

One of the hardest things for any writer to describe is a person. Most people look alike and different at the same time. It is the differences that are important in a description. Good descriptions are built around trying to explain what sets one person apart from others.

When you describe a person, use the "Fellow Officer Arrest Test". Have you given your fellow officers enough information to identify a suspect for arrest? Or is your description so vague that it would give you grounds to arrest all of your fellow officers?

In order to describe people clearly, follow these guidelines:

1. **Look for distinctive features.**

   If you write that the suspect was a white male, 183 centimetres tall, wearing a blue coat, you have narrowed the field somewhat. However, there are many men matching this description. If you add that the suspect has a tattoo of a snake over half of his face, then you have narrowed the field considerably. While most distinctive features are not quite this different or obvious, look for features that will distinguish the individual from other people.

2. **Be specific.**

   The reader of your description is relying on you to give a complete description, and you must use specific words to form that picture. For example, if you write that the suspect has a moustache, the reader may not "see" the right kind of moustache. Even adding information about the type of moustache, such as handlebar, Fu Manchu, military, or bushy, may not give the reader a full picture without information about the colour and texture of the hair.

3. **Focus on details that cannot be easily changed.**

   Focus descriptions on things that are difficult for someone to change, especially if you are describing someone who is trying to evade police attention. For example, it is hard to change features such as the shape and colour of the eyes, the size and shape of the ears, the scalp line, and the basic shape of the face.

In general, use the following headings to form the basis of descriptions of people:

1. **Name**

   Make sure the name is spelled correctly, and include any known aliases or nicknames.

2. **Race**

   Describe ethnic origin specifically. The common designations are

   White (wht.) or Caucasian (Cauc.)
   Black (blk.)
   Hispanic (His.), Mexican (Mex.)
   Aboriginal (Ab.)

Oriental (O.)

3. Sex

Indicate the person's sex. This is especially important when the name is "non-gender specific", such as Pat or Chris.

4. Age

Follow the form preferred by your department for listing the date of birth. Some police departments prefer a numerical designation, in which case the correct order is month, day, and year (01/02/47). Other departments prefer the date to be written out. In this case, the order may change according to service regulations or procedure. For example, some departments use 02 Jan. 1947, while other departments prefer January 2, 1947. Approximate age should be given using years of age. For example, "approx. 40 to 45 years of age".

5. Height and Weight

In Canada, height should be given in centimetres and weight should be given in kilograms. Refer to the metric tables, often printed in notebooks, for conversions.

6. Hair

Hair can be described by its texture, length, colour, and style. Also, note any absence of hair, such as a receding hairline or a bald spot. Facial hair can also be described by texture, length, colour, and style. Hair style is described as curly, wavy, short, long, dyed, ponytail, brush cut, toupee/wig, or "other". Specific style names, such as "buzz cut" or "mushroom top" can be used if you are sure that all of your readers will understand the specific description.

7. Eyes

Include a precise description of eye shape and colour. Note whether or not the person usually wears glasses or contact lenses.

8. Complexion

Complexions are usually described as dark, light/fair, sallow, ruddy, freckled, moles, or pimples/pockmarked. Again, it is important to be as specific as possible.

9. Outstanding Features

These could include any marks, scars, amputations, or tattoos. The description of a specific manner of walk, such as "staggered gait" or "limp on left leg", can also be helpful when identifying someone at a distance.

The most complete descriptions of people are needed for missing persons reports. (See the example of a Missing Persons Report in the Appendix to find all of the categories required.)

(b) Describing Events

Another type of description required for the narrative section is the description of events. To describe events:

1. Use chronological order.

Before you write an accurate description of events, you need to get a proper time sequence. Events must be arranged in the order in which they occurred, not in the order in which they were described to you.

2. Keep the names of the "players" clear.

When there are a number of people involved in an event, it is important to be able to tell "who's who" without a programme. Watch for the problems created by duplicate names. For example, if Mary and Harry Brown are involved in an incident, confusion will occur if you just refer to BROWN. Pronouns also cause confusion in descriptions unless the pronouns are used carefully. For example, "SMITH gave his gun to JONES and told him to take it to his place." Too many "he" pronouns result in confusion about possession. It is better to repeat a name than to use too many pronouns. Stylish writing is less important than clear writing in a police report.

(c) Describing Property

Use the acronym WANTED as a mnemonic to help you to remember the types of details you need to describe property:

W — What	What is it?
A — Appearance	What does it look like?
N — Number	How many articles are there? How many pieces are included? Are there any identifying numbers?
T — Type	What is the make or model?
E — Extraordinary	What special features will help to identify this object?
D — Dollars	How much is it worth?

3. REPORT WRITING STYLE

Good writing is simple writing. The purpose of the police report is to give information, not to impress the reader with a fancy writing style. Save "dawn was breaking over the squalid city" for your novel. In the report, write clearly.

Over the years, police writing has become associated with the use of a "police vocabulary". Like many other professions, law enforcement has its own particular jargon which, like the jargon of other fields, is used because it fosters a sense of group identity and becomes a type of shorthand for those who understand the terms and how they are used. Talk to police officers from anywhere in North America and you will find them salting their conversation with the same favourite "police phrases". For example, why does an officer always "proceed" somewhere? It is easier to write or say "went" or "drove", but "proceed" is part of the jargon, the language of policing. Another favourite word is "utilize". It would be easier to write "use" rather than "utilize". Choosing the simpler word also minimizes the possibility of making spelling errors.

Unfortunately, "police language" can limit the officer's vocabulary and may inhibit the officer's ability to make an accurate word choice. It is easier to "slip into" the jargon than to use words that are more precise. Consider some of the following alternatives to the traditional police vocabulary. Notice how these alternatives are frequently a more precise and accurate use of language.

1. **"advised"**
   "Advised" should not be used as a synonym for "told" or "said". For example,

   He was advised to leave.

   could be changed to

   He was told to leave.

2. **"altercation"**
   "Altercation" usually means "fight". For example,

   The altercation began in the bar.

   could be changed to

   The fight began in the bar.

3. **"contacted"**
   "Contacted" does not describe how information was communicated. For example,

   He contacted the police officer.

   could mean

   He touched the police officer.
   He telephoned the police officer.
   He waved to the police officer.
   He wrote to the police officer.
   He yelled at the police officer.

4. **"detected"**
   "Detected" should not be used as a synonym for "saw". For example,

   I detected the suspect's car.

   could be changed to

   I saw the suspect's car.

5. **"indicated"**
   "Indicated" can mean many things, including "said", "nodded", "pointed". For example, change

   PETERSON indicated his disapproval.

   to

   PETERSON said, "This plan stinks."

   Change

Bob indicated agreement.

to

Bob merely nodded in agreement.

Change

Lloyd indicated the location of the safe.

to

Lloyd pointed to the safe.

6. "informed"

"Informed" is not precise. It is better to use "told". For example,

I informed the client about the error.

could be changed to

I told the client about the error.

7. "observed"

"Observed" is often incorrectly used for "saw". For example,

I observed the man stumble.

could be changed to

I saw the man stumble.

8. "proceeded"

"Proceeded" should not be a "catch-all" to describe all movements. Instead, describe the action more specifically. For example,

We proceeded to the corner of Mill and Main Streets.

could be changed to

We drove to the corner of Mill and Main Streets.

or

We walked to the corner of Mill and Main Streets.

9. "responded"

Like "proceeded", "responded" is a vague term. There are many different ways to respond. For example,

We responded to the call.

could be changed to

We answered the call.

or

We responded to the problem.

could be changed to

We solved the problem.

10. "utilized"

"Utilized" can be replaced with "used". For example,

Police must utilize resources efficiently.

could be changed to

Police must use resources efficiently.

Good police reports must be well written. A good writing style allows the reader to understand the information quickly, without being bogged down by awkward wording or difficult sentences. A good writing style can be achieved by following these guidelines:

1. Keep sentences short.

Long sentences are hard to understand and increase the chances of making grammatical errors.

2. Begin each sentence with the subject.

Many sentence structure errors occur when sentences start with introductory phrases. It is easier for the reader to find the important information when the subject of the sentence is given first. For example,

Introductory Phrase:

After the fight in the parking lot, SMITH was arrested.

Subject First:

SMITH was arrested after the fight in the parking lot.

3. Keep pronoun references clear.

Pronouns refer to the closest preceding noun. Confusion occurs when the pronoun reference is not clear. For example,

The judge agreed that he was impaired when the accused committed the assault.

Who was impaired? The "he" in the sentence refers to "the judge", which is the closest noun preceding the pronoun. Confusion may also occur when there are too many pronouns in a sentence. For example,

> Lydia told her that her boss called and she left the message that she should clean out her desk.

When clarity is essential, repeat names rather than use too many pronouns.

4. Use active verbs.

Write sentences so that the verb describes the action of the subject, rather than something which is happening to the subject. Verbs that describe something which is happening to the subject are called "passive" verbs. Verbs that describe what the subject is doing are called "active" verbs. For example,

> Passive verb: The man was bitten by the dog.
> Active verb: The dog bit the man.

Active verbs also reduce the number of words in the sentence. Remember that shorter sentences are easier for the reader to understand.

5. Avoid uncommon abbreviations or slang.

The reader should not have to break your personal abbreviation code in order to understand the report. For example, if you are referring to a company when writing your report, use either the full word "company" or the common abbreviation "Co.". Using your own variation, like "comp." or "com'ny", causes confusion. Slang is not appropriate for reports, unless you are quoting the exact words of a speaker. For example,

> BURNS said, "I sold him a dime but he didn't pay up, so I took him out."

6. Keep language objective.

Use objective language to describe events and people. If you write "The stupid victim left his car door unlocked" or "She was wearing a provocative red dress", you are imposing your own opinions on the situation. This will weaken both your report and your courtroom presentation.

7. Use non-gender specific language.

Whenever possible, keep your language non-gender specific. For example, use "work-force" rather than "manpower", "sales clerk" rather than "salesgirl", and "firefighter" rather than "fireman". Avoid using feminine endings for words. Instead of "authoress", use "author"; instead of "executrix", use "executor". Language should reflect the fact that "manager", "administrator", "doctor", "lawyer", "secretary", and other job designations can be used to describe either men or women.

4. USING FIRST PERSON OR THIRD PERSON IN REPORTS

Whether you should use the first person or the third person in your reports will be determined by the style your police department prefers.

Another authority to deal with in determining the style will be the Crown attorney or prosecutor. This is particularly evident when preparing a Crown brief or documents for prosecution of a case. In some jurisdictions, Crown attorneys prefer the witness evidence to be submitted exactly as it may have been given for a witness statement, which will involve use of the first person. This method can cause confusion should you, as the reporting officer, need to add to the witness statement. In other jurisdictions, the style requested for all documents, including your own evidence, may be third person, so that consistency is maintained throughout the document.

Each style has advantages and disadvantages. First person style uses "I", "me", and "my" or "we", "us", and "our". For example,

> I saw YOUNG arrive at the school. ULRICH told me that YOUNG was carrying a concealed weapon. My partner, Constable BARRY, called for assistance.

First person is a more natural writing style than third person. It is easy to read in court and may add to the credibility of your observations by clearly showing that you were involved in the situation. First person is also easy to read because it requires less repetition of names.

However, first person style may be confusing if the report is submitted by more than one officer. In addition, the narrative section of the report may not be easily transferred to other documents, such as the Crown brief, when it is written in first person. Since first person also shows the officer's involvement, some supervisors believe that the report is more credible when it is written in third person.

In third person, writers give their names and use the pronouns "his" or "her". For example,

> Sergeant MELROSE saw YOUNG arrive at the school. ULRICH told MELROSE that YOUNG was carrying a concealed weapon. MELROSE'S partner, Constable BARRY, called for assistance.

Third person distances the writer from involvement in the situation, and it clearly identifies all of the people involved. As well, the reader does not have to refer to another part of the report in order to remember who is writing it. However, third person is awkward to write because it is not usual to use phrases like "the writer" or to use your name rather than "I".

5. COMPUTER-AIDED REPORT WRITING

Police departments are continuing to computerize their reporting systems. Mobile data terminals, laptop computers or desktop terminals allow officers to type their own reports directly into the main computer system. This reduces paperwork, and since reports will likely be filed almost immediately rather than at the end of a shift, they will be more accurate. With the trend to replace mobile data terminals with laptop computers, there is the additional advantage of being connected with the internal police network or intranet for accessing mug shots of known criminals as well as fingerprints. The laptop computers also improve the ability of police officers to search directly for criminal record information, outstanding warrants, and information on missing persons and stolen property on such databases as the Canadian Police Information Centre (CPIC), the Automated Canada United States Police Information Exchange System (ACUPIES) and the U.S.-based database of the National Crime Information Centre (NCIC), which is an FBI-sponsored agency. In order to use this computerized system to full advantage, you need to adapt your writing habits to this technology.

For example, good typing skills are important for officers using terminals. The "hunt and peck" system of typing is time-consuming and frustrating. You will save time in the long run if you improve your keyboarding skills either by taking a course or by using one of the self-teaching software packages.

It is especially important to plan your report before you start to enter it into the computer. Once you are using a shared system, you may prevent other officers from submitting their reports until you are finished. If you tie up the terminal while you try to think, organize, plan, and write, this will make the entire system less efficient. Make complete notes first, then type in your report.

Remember that the strength of any word processing system is that it allows you to edit and change what you have written. Typing speed can be increased because there is no need to worry about spoiling a page with a typographical error. However, increased typing speed can result in sloppy errors if you are not careful. Learn to use any editing features that your system may include, such as delete, block moves, or insert functions. However, the report will not edit itself, no matter how good the computer system. It is essential to take the time to re-read and edit what you have written before you press the final Enter key.

Another computerized system of reporting used in some areas is a phone-in report. Officers phone the report to a data terminal operator who types the report into the computer as it is dictated. To improve the quality of reports written this way, officers and the data terminal operator must work as a team. The officer can help the operator by following these steps:

1. Be prepared before you phone. Have all of the required names, dates, addresses, and descriptions in front of you. Writing out the narrative also helps, since you may be asked to repeat a word or phrase. This is difficult if you are composing as you dictate.

2. Speak slowly and clearly. Spell out any difficult or unusual words or names. Indicate where you would like punctuation or capitals to appear.

3. Listen carefully when the report is read back to you. Verify the information by referring to the notes you used when you were dictating. Remember, even though you do not see the report in front of you, it is still your report and your responsibility. The data operator is not there to compose or correct the report for you. Those duties still rest with the officer submitting the report.

6. SAMPLE REPORTS

The report forms reproduced in the Appendix will give you guidelines for the type of information and format required for different types of reports. While report forms may vary from one jurisdiction to another, these samples show general headings and document design.

2

The Notebook

1. THE IMPORTANCE OF THE NOTEBOOK

The notebook, or memo book, is one of the most important documents written by a police officer. In fact, it is the notebook that eventually puts criminals behind bars by providing the facts and details needed for further investigation and for court.

Police departments require the notebook to be a complete and accurate record of the actions and observations of an officer while on duty. The notebook is an official legal document that contains the details of an officer's investigations. Since it is a legal requirement that officers keep notes in the performance of their duties, notes can also be an exception to the hearsay evidence rules and may be used in court if the officer is unable to give the testimony. Therefore, it is critical that the information in the notebook be complete and accurate.

Good notes also help you to remember the details of events. With a large number of cases being investigated at the same time and the lengthy delays before cases are brought to trial, it is impossible to remember all of the names, dates, descriptions, and statements. The notebook overcomes the lapses in memory associated with the inevitable time-lag between an arrest and a trial. Without the notebook, the facts of an occurrence may be forgotten or distorted as one case becomes confused with another.

In addition, time constraints may prevent reports from being filled out immediately after each occurrence. Therefore, the notebook may serve as the only reliable record of events until the reports can be completed. You cannot trust memory alone.

The notebook is not the private property of the officer; in fact, the notebook is the property of the police department. For the preparation of their cases, the Crown attorney and the defence lawyer can see the notebook before the trial, or it can be examined during a trial by the lawyers, the judge, or the jury. With the court's permission, witnesses may also refer to the officer's notebook. Therefore, the notebook should not contain any "personal" notes that could be embarrassing.

2. KEEPING GOOD NOTES

Your department will issue a notebook, and it must be maintained in accordance with departmental regulations. The specific preferred format will be detailed in Operational or Administrative Procedures and must be followed exactly.

Generally, the information listed below will be included in the notebook. On the inside cover of each book, include

1. your name;
2. your badge number;
3. your department;
4. the date the book was started (and the number of the book if you use a numbering sequence).

Each day, include

1. the date, including the day of the week;
2. the time of reporting for duty;
3. the weather conditions, updated by time of day as conditions change;
4. the name of the person who paraded you for duty;
5. the patrol district assigned;
6. relevant messages, local wanted or missing persons, and other announcements or information you will need to refer to while on duty;

7. all actions taken during your duty and their times;
8. the specific details of each action taken or incident in which you were involved while on duty;
9. observations made about people, places, vehicles, or events;
10. statements made by the accused or witnesses;
11. exact transcription of interviews;
12. the time you reported off duty;
13. your rank, signature, and badge number.

Keep your notebook organized and up-to-date. It serves both as a record of your actions and as a tool to evaluate your performance. If your department requires you to submit monthly performance logs, keeping these records as a running tally at the end of each day's notebook entry will help you to compile these statistics quickly and accurately. An officer who can keep a good notebook will be regarded as an asset to the department and to the judicial system.

To keep a good notebook, follow these guidelines if your department does not issue orders with another procedure:

1. If the front cover of your notebook contains a pre-printed form for you to fill in, do so as soon as you receive your book. If a form is not supplied, note your name, rank, and badge number on the front of each book. Also, include the name of your department and the date the book was started. When you finish the book, note the date of the last entry on the front cover of the book.
2. If the pages of your notebook are not numbered, number them as you begin each new page. Do not leave any pages in the book blank, and do not remove pages from the book.
3. As a general rule, fill in every line on the page. If lines are left blank, this may provide lawyers with an opportunity to discredit your notes or to suggest that you may have left other spaces blank and filled them in at a later time. If you want to keep incidents separate, draw a line through the blank space and initial it. If a page is only partially filled at the end of your shift, it is acceptable to draw a line and place a signature through the remaining portion of the page and start the next entry on the next page. Again, you must follow the preference of your jurisdiction and your department.
4. Make your entries in pen. If you make a mistake when you are recording information, place a single line through the incorrect information and initial the error at both ends. The incorrect infor-

mation should remain visible so that it is clear you have not made any attempt to "cover up" anything.

5. Update your notebook as events occur. Note the time of each entry in the left margin. If your department-issue notebook does not have a left margin, rule one in.
6. Enter specific rather than general information. A vague entry like "General Observation" is of little help if you are asked to recall the details of the area you observed. Instead of "General Observation", you could note that you "Observed traffic at the corner of King and Queen" or that you "Patrolled the Hillside Heights and Queensdale Collegiate area."
7. If a witness writes a statement in your notebook, record the date and time of the statement and have the witness sign the statement in case he or she becomes hostile at a later time. Then, since the statement was signed, it may be used by the Crown attorney to cross-examine the witness in a trial.

   If the statement is from the accused, make sure that the accused reads the statement, and ask him or her to sign it. If the accused does not want to sign the statement, ask him or her to initial any mistakes. It is also extremely important that the statement have the time it was started and the time it was finished. These times will be crucial for a *voir dire*.

   If you are recording information from a complainant (especially in a domestic dispute), have the complainant read your notes and sign or initial each page. The signed statement will be important if, at a later time, the person decides not to pursue the complaint.
8. The notebook should be neat, and the writing in it must be legible. Remember that the notebook is not only for your personal use. Unless you are going to use universally recognized shorthand symbols, write everything out in full. Standard English short forms, such as Co. for company, are acceptable in notes; however, if you use "police short forms" such as A.R. (Armed Robbery), or B.E.& T. (Break, Enter, and Theft), make sure that you are using abbreviations familiar to ALL police officers in your jurisdiction.
9. Remember that the notebook contains confidential information. Always keep your notebook with you, and do not allow unauthorized people to read it. When giving evidence in court, put an elastic band around pages that are not relevant to the case under discussion.
10. Do not include any information in your notebook that is not relevant

to your duties. For example, shopping lists or personal telephone numbers should not be included. If you need to copy down personal information while you are on duty, use another sheet of paper.

11. If your notebook is lost, report the loss to your supervisor immediately.

It is essential that notes are made of every case or investigation. It is better to make complete notes of all investigations than to try to decide what information will be important at a later date. All details could be important. It is also essential that notes are recorded at the time of the events. This is supported in *R. v. Gwozdowski* (1972), 1972 CarswellOnt 944, [1973] 2 O.R. 50, 10 C.C.C. (2d) 434 (C.A.); and in *R. v. Woodcock* (1963), Crim. L. Rev. 273.

It is not acceptable to copy notes from another officer's notebook. However, you may check times or details with your partner in order to confirm your own recollection of the events. If you check information for your notes with your partner, mention this in your book and note that the information was the same as your partner's or that you had different recollections of time or events. Again, it is critical that you do not appear to be fabricating or covering up any information. This view is supported in *R. v. Vangent* (1978), 42 C.C.C. (2d) 313 (Ont. Prov. Ct.); and in *R. v. Marcello* (May 1984), Matlow Co. Ct. J. (Ont. Co. Ct.), at page 10.

Notetaking procedures and practices vary from one area to another. Often, the judges' rulings about what notes are acceptable in court govern how notes are taken. For example, in some areas it is acceptable for one officer to take notes while the other asks questions. After the interview, the officer who was questioning may read the notes and initial them in the notebook. In this way, the judge may allow notes to be used by both of the officers to refresh their memories in court. However, in other jurisdictions this practice is not allowed. Therefore, it is always a good habit to keep your own notes of every event and to record your own actions and observations. See the comments of Justice Salhany in *R. v. Charest*, summarized at (1981), 7 W.C.B. 86 (Ont. Co. Ct.). See also *R. v. Barrett* (1993), 1993 CarswellOnt 113, 23 C.R. (4th) 49 (Ont. C.A.) [reversed on other grounds, [1995] 1 S.C.R. 752, 38 C.R. (4th) 1, 96 C.C.C. (3d) 319 (S.C.C.)]; and *R. v. Green* (1998), 1998 CarswellOnt 3820 (Ont. Gen. Div.).

Sample Notebook Entry

Thursday, January 31, 2002
8:00 a.m. to 4:00 p.m. shift
Patrol area: 22-2-40
Cloudy, mild, 16 C.
Roads: dry
10-70: M. W. 25 yrs, Brn, Brn,
blue jacket, jeans, white runners, limp rt. leg, tattoo on rt. elbow of red snake
Wanted for A.R. — Friday, 30-06-90, 03:00 hrs at Queen Variety, armed with a knife
08:00 paraded by Sgt. Wood
portable radio 1132
08:05 vehicle check — car 162
08:08 10-8 patrol 22-2-40
08:15 Radio Call — 3896
Humberlane Drive
Big Man Tires, B.&E.
08:20 10-7
spoke to Mr. George Mann. . . .
. . . . (continue with the details of the investigation)

3. RECORD COMPLETE INFORMATION

Information in the notebook must be complete and accurate. Remember that it is easier to obtain this information at the time of the occurrence than to gather the information later. Without complete and accurate information, it will be difficult to fill out reports or to give evidence at a later time. To ensure that the information in the notebook is complete and accurate, follow these guidelines for gathering the descriptive information that will be needed in your report:

1. People

name (aliases and nicknames);
age (including date of birth);
address (note the difference between a mailing address and a residence address; also include the postal code, lot and concession numbers, property or fire number, and township or county for

rural addresses; also note the directions for the house location or a description of the house for rural addresses);
home phone number (including area code);
marital status (and name of spouse, if appropriate);
social insurance number;
driver's licence number (and issuing province);
occupation;
place of employment;
business phone number;
sex;
race;
height;
weight;
build (slender, medium, heavy);
hair colour;
eye colour;
physical/mental condition;
scars, tattoos, marks, outstanding features;
clothing (if needed for identification);
and, if the person is a potential witness, find out if the person has any vacation plans and also obtain the name of the next of kin, if possible, complete with addresses and phone numbers.

2. Vehicles

owner's name;
licence number;
licence year;
licence province;
licence validation tag number;
vehicle year;
make;
model;
style;
colour;
vehicle identification number;
customized options (roof rack, mud flaps, etc.);
make of radio, speakers, tires, etc.;
description of vehicle contents;
present value;

condition of vehicle (good, fair, rough, restored, like new, etc.);
keys (how many keys were there and where are they?).

3. **Bicycles**
owner's name and address;
make;
model name and number;
serial number;
size and colour of frame;
equipment (including light, bell, kickstand, carrier);
identifying marks;
licence number (if one exists);
value.

4. **Clothing**
type of article;
style;
approximate date of purchase;
value at the time of purchase, and present value;
size;
fabric;
colour;
trimmings;
rips, tears, or stains;
manufacturer's labels, and other labels;
description of what, if anything, was in the pockets.

5. **Jewelry**
type of article;
date and place of purchase;
value at the time of purchase;
present value, and where and when it was appraised;
metal (including carat number for gold);
size;
type, number, and size of stones;
engravings, inscriptions, markings;
manufacturer;
age;
unusual features;
picture, if available.

6. Furniture

type of article;
style;
material — type of wood or fabric;
number of pieces;
manufacturer;
distinctive features or marks;
value at time of purchase and present value.

7. Appliances or Electrical Equipment

type of article;
age of article;
brand name;
model, size;
serial number;
colour;
material;
identifying marks;
value at time of purchase and present value.

8. Road Conditions

weather conditions affecting road;
direction of road (east–west, north–south);
volume of traffic on road (general light, high between 3:30 p.m. to 4:00 p.m.);
surface type;
width of road, width of shoulder, curbs or ditches;
grade;
unusual characteristics;
hazards;
marks on road;
street lights.

9. Weapons

type of weapon (revolver, shotgun, knife);
quantity (each type described separately);
manufacturer;
model;
calibre;
age;

serial number (if visible or indicate if filed off);
finish;
distinctive features (initials, inscriptions);
origin, if it can be determined (stolen, purchased, home-made);
value.

10. Additional Descriptors

Police officers, just as other people, "feel" or sense certain "things" that may evoke a particular response. In police work, that feeling or sensation is often called a "hunch" or "gut feeling". Saying that you had a "hunch" while giving evidence to explain your actions is not sufficient. You will need to be more specific and detailed in your evidence and in your notes. This is especially important when attempting to establish reasonable grounds or persuading the court that an action was not taken arbitrarily. Recording this information immediately in your notes can go a long way in establishing your credibility before the courts.

Recording specific actions are self-evident, such as those that would be required to establish impairment. However, police officers often overlook the recording of other evidence that can be just as important. Non-verbal communication or body language is extremely important for officer safety and can also be relevant evidence that the court may wish to hear. An often used phrase in officer safety is "when the body language and the words spoken are in conflict, trust the body language first". Learn to identify and record those actions that caused you to have that "hunch". Examples of these observations may include:

continually swallowed hard before responding to a question
clenched his right hand so that knuckles became white
would adjust his glasses before answering a question relevant to guilt
pupils were constricted
beads of perspiration were visible on his brow
was continually moving his feet while talking
would look up and to the right when answering a difficult question
breaths were short and shallow
kept looking around

By themselves, these observations may mean nothing and are often overlooked. Under the right circumstances, these observations can speak volumes. Properly recorded in your notes and given in evidence later, the observations may allow others to form the same "feeling" or opinion that you experienced.

4. USE OF NOTES IN COURT

The notebook is invaluable when presenting evidence in court. Cases can take months or even years to reach the courts; after such a long delay, it will be difficult to recall all of the information regarding a specific occurrence unless an accurate and detailed record of the incident is available. The notes demonstrate that the officer is a professional who knows how to properly document an investigation.

Notes can also be used to record statements of witnesses, victims or suspects. These statements can be used in court to refresh their memories about what happened or to revive their memories when they have no recollection of events. There are several cases to support the use of the notebook in this way: *R. v. Booth* (1984), 1984 CarswellBC 367, 58 B.C.L.R. 63, 15 C.C.C. (3d) 237 (C.A.); *R. v. Bengert* (1978), 1978 CarswellBC 529, (*sub nom. R. v. Bengert (No. 5)*) 15 C.R. (3d) 21, (*sub nom. R. v. Bengert (No. 2)*) [1979] 1 W.W.R. 472 (B.C.S.C.), affirmed (1980), 15 C.R. (3d) 114, 1980 CarswellBC 439, (*sub nom. R. v. Bengert (No. 5)*) 53 C.C.C. (2d) 481 (B.C.C.A.), leave to appeal to S.C.C. refused (1980), 53 C.C.C. (2d) 481n (S.C.C.). Note that the Kaufmann Inquiry's recommendations included the videotaping or audiotaping of suspects and police videotaping of designated witnesses (Recommendations, 96-98, *The Commission on Proceedings Involving Guy Paul Morin*).

The notebook may also be used as the basis of cross-examination on prior inconsistent statements. This could occur if you had taken a statement from a witness, but later he or she claimed to have no memory of the event or gave inconsistent evidence. With the permission of the court, the original statement in your notebook, signed by the witness at the time it was taken, could be used for cross-examination by the Crown attorney. The procedure for this type of application is outlined in section 9(2) of the *Canada Evidence Act*, R.S.C. 1985, c. C-5. This is further supported by case law in *R. v. Milgaard,* 1971 CarswellSask 26, 14 C.R.N.S. 34, [1971] 2 W.W.R. 266, 2 C.C.C. (2d) 206 (Sask. C.A.), leave to appeal to S.C.C. refused (1971), 4 C.C.C. (2d) 566n

(S.C.C.). See also *R. v. Rouse* (1978), (*sub nom. McInroy v. R.*) [1979] 1 S.C.R. 588, 5 C.R. (3d) 125.

In *R. v. Carpenter* (1982), 1982 CarswellOnt 97, 31 C.R. (3d) 261, the Ontario Court of Appeal held that a conversation consisting of questions asked by a police officer and answers given by a person who later was a witness, which was recorded as translated by the officer at the time, falls within the meaning of "a statement . . . reduced to writing" under section 9(2) of the *Canada Evidence Act*. However, in *R. v. Handy* (1978), 1978 CarswellBC 515, 5 C.R. (3d) 97 (B.C.C.A.), followed in *R. v. Cassibo* (1982), 1982 CarswellOnt 850, 70 C.C.C. (2d) 498 (Ont. C.A.), the court held that a police officer's notes of an interview with a witness that were neither confirmed nor verified by the witness could not be considered as a statement in writing or reduced to writing such as to fall under section 9(2).

To improve your testimony as a witness in court, read your notes before testifying. Once you are on the stand, you do not want to struggle to understand your own handwriting or to piece together the information you recorded months earlier. Reading the notes beforehand allows you to familiarize yourself with the details of the case.

When you are on the stand and want to refer to your notes, ask the judge's permission. When that permission is granted, thank the judge before opening your notebook. Do not read your notes word for word. Instead, refer to them for specific details, such as the spelling of names, or for exact addresses, or to refresh your memory about the sequence of events.

A good investigation is based on how well you can observe details. Unless the details are recorded completely and accurately in your notes, your investigation will not be complete. Poor notes lead to poor reports. Poor notes also undermine your credibility in court. It is worth the extra time to make notebook entries complete and correct. The details recorded in the notebook are the foundation on which every aspect of the case depends. Make sure that these notes provide a strong foundation for every investigation.

3

Internal Memos and Emails

Within every organization, the primary purpose of memos or emails is to keep information flowing up, down, and across the chain of command. Emails are effective for day-to-day communications. Memos have become more formal and are used when a permanent record of the communication needs to be on the books. Generally, the guidelines for writing memos and emails are the same. Memos provide a permanent record of events and are especially important for documenting items such as reprimands and commendations. Memos or emails are often sent as a follow-up to a conversation. A listener may forget or misunderstand what was said, but with a memo the exact words are printed and available for reference at any time. Another important function of memos or emails is the distribution of the same information to a wide audience. Announcements about meetings, or revisions to policies and procedures, can be made in emails to ensure that everyone gets the same information at the same time.

For memos to serve as useful records, however, a system must be developed to file the memos received and the ones sent. Never send a memo without keeping a copy for your own files. It is also important that memos not be overused. An avalanche of repetitive or uninformative memos or emails simply creates more work for you and your co-workers.

Finally, on a personal level, the memo is an excellent method of enhancing your professional image. Your memos may be read by someone who is not familiar with your work. In such a situation, the memo can create the image that will be associated with your name. In order to create the right image, you need to provide information to the reader in a clear and concise manner.

1. MEMO FORMAT

Most police departments have pre-printed forms for memos. These forms simplify the format of the memo by providing spaces for the appropriate headings. To fill in these headings correctly, follow the procedures of your department. If there are no established procedures, use these guidelines:

The standard headings of a memo are

TO:	Use the recipient's rank and full name, or the recipient's full name and job title. Be sure to spell the name correctly. For example, Staff Sergeant Bronwyn Cavanagh Julia Westlake, Personnel Director
FROM:	Use your rank and full name, or your full name and job title. For example, Constable Marilyn Malefski Janice Rosenburg, Graduate Student Advisor
RE (or SUBJECT):	Identify the subject of the memo exactly. Use specific subject headings whenever possible. For example, it is better to use "Guidelines for Submitting Expense Claims" than "Expense Claims" because the first one identifies the subject. Simply giving "Expense Claims" forces the reader to look further into the memo to see what information is being discussed.

DATE: Write the date in full or use the notation system recognized by your department (*e.g.*, March 15, 1999 or 01/06/93).

If your department does not have a standard format for memos or emails, these headings provide a useful guideline. Generally, the headings for emails will be built into the software.

The headings are the easiest part of the memo. Once the headings have been completed, you must concentrate on sending the right message to the reader. As with any other kind of writing, a good memo or email requires planning, drafting, revising, and proofreading. If you assume that because a memo is short you can just write it "off the top of your head", you will find that this practice can make writing difficult. As well, it is possible that the reader may misunderstand the message you intended to deliver.

2. PLANNING THE MEMO OR EMAIL

In order to plan your message, consider the information the memo or email must contain. Make a list of everything that you think the memo should include. This gives you the opportunity to gather the correct and complete information that you will need to organize your message. Once you have gathered the information you need to include, concentrate on how to transmit that information effectively.

Write a point-form outline using the information you have listed. Start the outline by listing your main point so that you can keep everything else in the memo focused on that point. This will remind you to put the most important idea first in the final memo so that even a busy reader cannot miss it. Remember, your memo should not be patterned after a mystery novel in which the important information is revealed to the reader at the end.

Anyone who has to read memos prefers writers who get to the point quickly. Organize information on your outline in the order of what the reader a) needs to know, b) wants to know, and c) likes to know. Remember to organize according to your reader's priorities, not your own.

As you develop your outline, consider the purpose of your memo or email. What do you want the memo to accomplish? If you are simply giving information, then the purpose of the memo is to transmit that information clearly. If you want the reader to take action based on the memo, decide what action the reader is to take. Have you provided all of the information the reader needs to take that action or to make the right decision? Have you made it easy for the reader to take action by providing the necessary phone numbers, dates, or names? Does the reader know what action you want taken? A good memo relies on clarity, and a good outline ensures that your message will be clear.

3. WRITING THE MEMO OR EMAIL

Once you have made an outline of the information to be included and have arranged it in the most effective order, think about who will read your memo or email. Successful writing is tailored to the reader. Consider how much the reader already knows about the topic so that you do not waste time covering the obvious, or worse, omitting necessary explanations.

In most cases, you are writing an internal memo; consequently, your readers will be other police personnel. It is, therefore, acceptable to use familiar police terms and expressions. However, avoid using jargon or abbreviations with which your reader may not be familiar. It is always safer to use the correct terms and expressions so that the reader does not have to ask for clarification.

Even if you know your reader, keep the tone of your memo formal. Keep in mind that even though you may have a single reader on the memo heading, memos are read by many different readers. A memo is no place for jokes or references to personal events. Many departments have specific policies against sending jokes or other personal information in an email. As well, do not use memos to express anger. The memo you dashed off in anger ultimately could do more to harm you than to correct the situation that has upset you. In addition to being formal, the memo should be polite. Too many memo writers end up being officious, when what they want to be is official. An official tone is not rude.

The body of the memo should be written using clearly developed paragraphs. In general, the opening paragraph gives the most important information; the following paragraphs provide explanation; and the final paragraph indicates what action the reader should take. If the paragraphs in your memo are too short, the memo sounds "choppy". It is important that even an email be coherent and clearly developed. If the paragraphs are too long, the reader is overwhelmed by the amount of information. While memos can be any length, from a few paragraphs to many pages, it is essential that the information be given clearly so that the reader can understand the information after reading the memo once.

As you write, remember the ABC's of good memos.

A. Accurate

The memo or email must contain correct information. Mistakes in spelling or grammar could confuse your reader. Mistakes in times, dates or names ruin the effectiveness of the memo. Check your memo carefully for accuracy.

B. Brief

Do not try to impress the reader with your vocabulary or with your vast knowledge about the topic. Include only the information that is essential. Get to the point quickly.

C. Complete

Answer all of the reader's questions. Provide all of the details so that you do not have to send a second memo to supplement the information given in the first one. Include all information that will make it easy for the reader to respond or take action.

4. TYPES OF MEMOS

(a) Informational Memo

The informational memo is organized using the following pattern:

1. Announce the news.
2. Give the details.

3. Add further explanations.
4. Give a contact for further information, if needed.

For example,

TO: All Sergeants
FROM: Staff Sergeant Mary Sheppard
RE: Essay Writing Course
DATE: April 4, 2002

The training department will now offer an essay writing course as part of our in-service curriculum. If you are planning to write promotional essays or to take college courses, the essay writing course offered by the training department will help you.

The course is three hours long and is offered on the following dates:
June 21 — 15:00 to 18:00 hours
July 10 — 08:00 to 11:00 hours
August 22 — 13:00 to 16:00 hours

Please register before JUNE 5, 2002, for the course that is most convenient for you. Registration forms are available in the Training Department office.

If you would like any additional information, please call ext. 4575.

(b) Explanation Memo

These memos are often jokingly referred to as "Dear Chief" memos (even though they are not always written to the chief). They can be difficult to write because the writer is faced with explaining some problem or accounting for actions taken. A good organizational plan is:

1. Apologize and describe the problem.
2. Explain what caused the problem.
3. Explain your role in the situation.
4. Describe what you have done to solve the problem.
5. Describe what actions the reader needs to take, if any.
6. Give a contact for further information, if needed.

For example,

TO: Staff Sergeant Frederick Hunt, Training Department
FROM: Constable John Gage, Badge # 1302
RE: Absence from class on September 21
DATE: October 8, 2001

Please accept my apology for missing the class on Time Management on September 21. My car skidded on the ice on Garrison Road and struck a telephone pole. I was not injured but had to wait for the tow truck. Unfortunately, the weather conditions caused many other accidents and the truck took over two hours to arrive. After my car was towed home, I called a taxi, which arrived an hour later.

Although I made every effort to arrive as quickly as possible, I missed the morning session. I have received all of the notes from Constable Quigley, and she has discussed them with me. I understand that I am still responsible for this material for the examination.

Please let me know if there is anything else I should do to compensate for missing this class. I can be contacted in the Training office until October 25.

(c) Suggestion or Recommendation Memo

If you have good ideas for changes you would like the supervisor to consider, use this plan:

1. Briefly describe the existing system.
2. Point out the flaws in the system.
3. Explain how the problems could be solved.
4. Offer to make the changes, or to contribute to the success of the new system.
5. Explain how the reader can make the necessary changes easily.

Remember that the success of this type of memo rests on the tone you use. The tone must be helpful, not demanding. For example,

TO: Inspector Sarah Wallace
FROM: Sergeant Peter Revell
RE: New Printer for the Fraud Office
DATE: September 5, 2001

The printer that we use in the Fraud office has broken down six times in the past two days. It is a dot matrix Perfpro model that has been discontinued by the manufacturer. This makes parts expensive and difficult to get. The printer malfunctions are causing us delays in processing our reports and in clearing our cases.

Please consider the advantage of moving one of the laser printers from the Identification Unit to our office. Identification has four laser printers; however, they are rarely all used at the same time. Moving one of the printers would not disrupt their unit, and it would certainly help ours.

If you agree that one of these printers could be moved, I would be happy to train the members of our office in the operation of the printer to ensure that it is properly used and maintained.

Please call me at ext. 313 to discuss how this move could be arranged. Thank you for your consideration of this suggestion.

(d) Commendation or "Job Well Done" Memo

When someone has done a good job, use this pattern to give a commendation:

1. Give the congratulations.
2. Describe the event.
3. Explain the benefit to the individual or to the department.
4. Repeat the congratulations.

For example,

TO: Constable Tim Ng
FROM: Staff Sergeant Richard Yarbrough
RE: Fund Raising Success
DATE: May 13, 2002

Congratulations on the success of the golf tournament. It was quite an accomplishment to raise over $8,000 and to exceed last year's total by 15%. I know that the participants in the tournament enjoyed themselves, and the Neighbourhood Watch Safety Program will be improved by the increased funding.

Without your organizational skills, enthusiasm, and dedication, the golf tournament could not have been so successful. Thank you for all of your hard work.

(e) Reprimand Memo

If you must give a reprimand, use this pattern for organization:

1. Give a clear statement of the problem.
2. Explain why the actions resulted in a problem.
3. Explain the steps the individual must take to solve the problem.
4. Explain the steps the writer or the supervisor is taking to solve the problem.
5. Explain what will happen if the problem is not solved.
6. Close with a clear statement of resolution.

For example,

TO: Constable Jeff Graham
FROM: Sergeant Willis Hayes
RE: Parking in the Visitor Area
DATE: April 12, 2002

Please stop parking your car in the Visitor parking area. Your actions reduce our very limited parking spaces for the public and cause more traffic problems in the parking lot.

I have asked you to move your car on three occasions. This morning, you parked in the Visitor area again and had to be told to move your car. In the future, you must park in the Employee parking area behind the station.

If your car is found in the Visitor area again, I have authorized Ms. Fairfield to have the car towed to our impound lot on Culver Street. In addition, if you do not follow the parking procedure, you could lose your parking privileges and have to find space for your car elsewhere.

I trust we will have no more problems and that you understand that your car must not be parked in the Visitor parking area at any time.

(f) Request for Approval Memo

In order to get your requests or proposals approved, follow this organizational plan:

1. State what you would like the reader to do.
2. Explain your request, providing details.
3. Explain how approving your request would benefit the department.
4. Provide a clear explanation of the action the reader should take to indicate approval.
5. Provide a contact to answer additional questions, if needed.

For example,

TO: Sergeant David Ward
FROM: Constable Kathy Milford
RE: Approval for Supervisory Training Course
DATE: March 11, 2002

Please approve this request to allow me to take the Supervisory Training course offered from July 10 to July 12. This course is offered by our Training Department. The course will help me to build my skills and develop the supervisory techniques I need for my new position as co-ordinator of the "Lunch Bunch Fitness Program". In addition, these supervisory skills will help me to be more effective in my patrol duties.

Please sign the enclosed registration form and return it to me before March 30. If you have any questions, please contact me during the "A" Shift or speak to Sergeant Wilder, our Training Counsellor. Thank you for your assistance.

Your memos and emails are a measure of how well you can communicate within your organization. Make sure that your memos reflect your attention to detail, your ability to organize information effectively, and your good writing skills.

PART TWO
A REFERENCE GUIDE FOR BETTER WRITING SKILLS

4

Spelling

1. THE IMPORTANCE OF GOOD SPELLING

The English language is not very co-operative when it comes to spelling. Take the sound of the letter "f", for example. In "phone", the sound is made by the letters "ph." The same sound in the word "tough" is formed by the letters "gh." The word "gruff", which rhymes with "tough", has two "f" 's.

It is easy to give in to the temptation to abandon all hope of spelling correctly. Fight that temptation. It may be difficult to spell correctly, but it is important. If you are able to spell correctly, you will spend less time doing paperwork. Stopping to check the spelling of words wastes time and distracts you from completing your work. In addition, incorrect spelling in a legal document could cause other, more serious complications. Legal documents must be accurate in all details.

Determining the accuracy of facts and issues in a case is complicated enough without the additional burden of spelling errors. For example, an error in the spelling of the name of an accused could make it difficult or even impossible to determine whether that accused was involved in other cases. If a street name is misspelled, time could be lost while the error is corrected. When a legal document contains spelling errors, the reader is forced to examine the writing itself rather than concentrate on the information being conveyed.

A spelling error could cause confusion and could make writing difficult to read. It could force the reader to act as an interpreter in order to translate a sentence such as "His bale was poestid by his fiend," to "His bail was posted by his friend." At its worst, a simple spelling error could change the meaning of a sentence completely (*e.g.*, "The accused was apprehended while breaking in to the paint shop" instead of "The accused was apprehended while breaking in to the *print* shop").

Spelling errors weaken your image and your credibility. Supervising officers will not see your day-to-day activities, but they will read what you have written about those activities. Whether or not your writing is an accurate reflection of your overall skills, it will be used to judge your professional competence. Make sure your writing reflects the same high standards that you maintain in every other aspect of your duties. Remember that spelling errors are the most obvious mistakes in written work. Some readers take perverse delight in finding spelling errors; others simply notice the errors with annoyance. Spelling errors are rarely overlooked or forgiven. Unfortunately, when a reader finds spelling errors, these errors cast suspicion on the accuracy of the information contained in the rest of the document.

2. A CAUTION: COMPUTER SPELL CHECK PROGRAMS

As more police departments computerize and train officers in the use of word processing programs, the reliance on spell check programs increases. Certainly, spell check programs can help writers to spot and correct spelling errors easily and quickly by providing instant access to an on-screen dictionary. While writers should be encouraged to take advantage of any technology that makes the task of writing faster and easier, the limitations of spell check programs should be recognized.

These programs do not verify the spelling of words that are not in their "software dictionaries". Street names, personal names, contractions, and technical or legal terms may not be included. Even if the dictionary can be modified, the words must be entered accurately or the spelling error will be propagated every time that word is checked by the spell check program. As well, these programs do not discriminate between the spelling variations of words determined by the context of the word within the sentence. For example, the program will accept both "principal" or "principle" as correct, and it will accept both the singular and plural of a word as correct. In addition, the computer may indicate errors when none exist. For example, if the word "layout" is checked, the program may flag the word as incorrect when, in fact, it is correct.

Canadians are faced with some unique spelling problems that cannot be solved by computer spell check programs. Some of these programs only give American spelling for words, while others only give British spelling. Canadian spelling is a blend of the two language traditions. For example, Canadians retain the British spelling of "colour", but reject the British spelling of "aluminium" in favour of the American "aluminum". Check the type of dictionary used by your word processing program. In some programs you can change from American to Canadian to British spelling.

Spell check programs provide the writer with another line of defence against errors. However, these programs are no substitute for "old-fashioned" spelling knowledge. While it is advisable to use all of the available technology, it is unwise to become dependent on it. Knowing how to spell is a skill that you must possess, whether you write with a pen or with a computer.

3. IMPROVE YOUR SPELLING

Once you understand the advantages of correct spelling, you can begin to improve your spelling by following these suggestions:

1. Improve your handwriting. If you do not write clearly, anything you write may appear to be misspelled.
2. Use a dictionary, or refer to the spelling list in this chapter. It is easier to refer to a dictionary than to memorize all of the correct spellings for all of the words in the English language.
3. Every time you look up the correct spelling of a word in your dictionary, put a check mark in the dictionary's margin beside the word. This will give you a strong visual reminder of the words that you use frequently and have trouble spelling.
4. To learn how to spell words, write them out correctly several times. This helps to "fix" the correct spelling in your mind.
5. Do not be confused by words that sound familiar but have different spellings and different meanings. (For more information about these words, see Chapter 5 on Usage in this book.)

6. Use memory devices (called "mnemonics") to help you remember correct spellings. For example, remember that "separate" contains two "a" 's in the middle by visualizing a golfer who is at "par" and who "ate" too much before his pants separated. Research indicates that mnemonics work most effectively when they are silly.
7. Think about what you are writing as you write it. Do not let your mind race ahead of your pen.
8. Pronounce words correctly to assist in visualizing the proper spelling. Many spelling errors are caused by poor pronunciation. For example, do not say "filum" for "film," or "atheletic" for "athletic".
9. Proofread your writing just for spelling. It is difficult to find errors in content, style, and spelling at the same time.
10. Do crossword puzzles. In addition to increasing your vocabulary, crossword puzzles demand accurate spelling because the words will not connect correctly if you make spelling errors.

Learning the common spelling rules will also help to improve your spelling. While there are exceptions to the rules, it is better to be right most of the time than to worry about the few exceptions. To learn spelling rules, develop a "spelling vocabulary". Here are the words used when spelling rules are explained:

Vowel
The letters "a," "e," "i," "o," and "u" (and sometimes "y").

Consonant
All of the other letters.

Syllable
The letter or letters that form one sound in a word. Each syllable will contain at least one vowel. You can hear syllables if you pronounce a word slowly. The "breaks" in the pronunciation are the syllables. If you say "policeman" slowly you will hear that it has three syllables — "po" "lice" "man".

Root
The basic element from which the word is formed. The root is usually a word. For example, in the word "disappearance","appear" is the root. "Dis" and "ance" have been added to it.

Prefix
Letters that are added to the beginning of a root. For example, "dis" is the prefix in the word "disappearance".

Suffix
Letters that are added to the end of a root. For example, "ance" is the suffix in the word "disappearance".

4. SOLVE SPELLING PROBLEMS: USE SPELLING RULES

1. When should you use "ei" or "ie"?

To help you remember which combination is correct, repeat the old rhyme:

> Use *i* before *e*
> Except after *c*
> Or for the sound *a*
> As in *neighbour* and *weigh.*

This rhyme will help you see that it is "i" before "e" in words like

> grieve, yield, mischief, brief, field.

It is "e" before "i" in words such as

> receive, conceive, deceit, perceive,

or to make the "a" sound in words such as

> eight, reindeer, vein, freight.

The combination "cien" is the exception to this old rhyme. The "sh" sound of the letters "cie" should alert you to this combination in words such as

> proficient, efficient, deficient, conscientious, sufficient.

Of course, there are other exceptions to the rule. Watch out for words such as

> codeine, counterfeit, caffeine, protein, height, seize.

2. How do you know if a word ends in "able" or "ible"?

Unfortunately, there is no general spelling rule to solve this problem. Your best defence is to memorize the spelling of "able" and "ible" words. For example,

"ABLE" WORDS	"IBLE" WORDS
acceptable	admissible
approachable	combustible
capable	contemptible
changeable	credible
commendable	defensible
defendable	incorrigible
identifiable	infallible
indictable	irresistible
inevitable	permissible
manageable	susceptible
predictable	
probable	

Invent your own memory aids for the words that cause you the most trouble. For example,

a) to remember the "able" at the end of "identifiable", remind yourself that you must be "able" to make the identification; and
b) to remember the "ible" at the end of "admissible" remind yourself: "I" will "miss" the admission if "I" arrive late.

3. How do you know if a word ends in "ence" or "ance"?

Again, there is no simple answer. Memorize the spelling of "ance" and "ence" words. For example,

"ANCE" WORDS	"ENCE" WORDS
acceptance	adolescence
assistance	competence
attendance	coherence
compliance	defence
continuance	deterrence
deviance	evidence
disappearance	negligence

endurance	obedience
grievance	offence
maintenance	patience
observance	sequence
reconnaissance	
reluctance	
significance	
vengeance	

Mnemonics will also help. For example,

a) to remember the "ance" at the end of significance, remember "a" significant event; and
b) to remember the "ence" at the end of "negligence", remind yourself that it makes "sense" to use the "e" in negligence.

4. How do you know if a word begins with "aq" or "acq"?

In general, words that refer to water begin with "aq". Notice this connection and spelling in words such as

aqua, aquarium, aquatic, aqueduct, Aquarius.

Other words that begin with the same sound usually begin with "acq", such as

acquaint, acquire, acquisition, acquit.
(Note the exception: *aquiline*.)

Also, remember that the letter "q" is always followed by the letter "u".

5. Does the spelling of the root of a word change when you add a prefix?

No. Prefixes should not cause spelling errors if you remember to keep all of the letters in the root of the word.

PREFIX	ROOT	CORRECT SPELLING
dis	arm	disarm
il	legal	illegal
mis	spell	misspell
un	necessary	unnecessary

6. Do you drop the final "e" in the root of a word when you add a suffix?

Drop the final "e" in the root of a word when you add a suffix that begins with a vowel.

ROOT	SUFFIX	CORRECT SPELLING
advise	able	advisable
argue	ing	arguing
assure	ance	assurance
charge	ed	charged
fate	al	fatal

Keep the final "e" in the root of a word when you add a suffix that begins with a consonant.

ROOT	SUFFIX	CORRECT SPELLING
forgive	ness	forgiveness
hope	ful	hopeful
nine	teen	nineteen
safe	ly	safely
state	ment	statement

Keep the final "e" in the root of the word if that root ends in "ce" or "ge" and if you are adding a suffix beginning with "a" or "o".

ROOT	SUFFIX	CORRECT SPELLING
change	able	changeable
courage	ous	courageous
notice	able	noticeable
outrage	ous	outrageous
peace	able	peaceable

Keep the final "e" in the root of the word if that root ends in "ee" or "oe".

ROOT	SUFFIX	CORRECT SPELLING
agree	able	agreeable
canoe	ing	canoeing
free	dom	freedom

Keep the final "e" in the root of the word, even before a suffix beginning with a vowel, if confusion with a similar word could result.

dye (to colour or tint) — dyeing
die (to cease to live) — dying

singe (to scorch) — singeing
sing (to vocalize music) — singing

Finally, there are some exceptions. Watch out for words such as

truly, argument, skiing, mileage, duly, judgement or judgment, acknowledgment or *acknowledgement.*

7. When do you double the final consonant in the root of a word if you are adding a suffix?

Double the final consonant in the root if

a) the word has only one syllable; and
b) the word ends in a single consonant after a single vowel; and
c) the suffix begins with a vowel.

ROOT	SUFFIX	CORRECT SPELLING
beg	ar	beggar
flip	ed	flipped
hit	ing	hitting
omit	ed	omitted
plan	ed	planned
permit	ing	permitting

8. When do you change the final letter "y" in the root of a word to an "i" before a suffix?

Change the final "y" in a root to an "i" if

a) it is preceded by a consonant; and
b) the suffix is NOT "ing", "ness", "ment", or "fil".

ROOT	SUFFIX	CORRECT SPELLING
baby	es	babies
beauty	ful	beautiful
heavy	er	heavier
penalty	es	penalties

Keep the final "y" in the root if it is preceded by a vowel.

ROOT	SUFFIX	CORRECT SPELLING
annoy	ance	annoyance
attorney	s	attorneys
obey	ed	obeyed
play	er	player

The exception to this rule occurs with the suffix "ly". When "ly" is added to a word ending in "y", the "y" is sometimes changed to "i".

ROOT	SUFFIX	CORRECT SPELLING
shy	ly	shyly
sly	ly	slyly
heavy	ly	heavily
weary	ly	wearily

9. If the root ends and the suffix begins with the same consonant, do you keep both consonants?

Yes. The root remains unchanged when this combination occurs.

ROOT	SUFFIX	CORRECT SPELLING
accidental	ly	accidentally

annual	ly	annually
mean	ness	meanness

10. How do you know whether you should use the suffix spelled "sede", "ceed", or "cede"?

a) "Supersede" is the only word that ends in "sede".
b) "Exceed", "proceed", and "succeed" are the only words that end in "ceed".
c) All of the other words with the same sound end in "cede", as in "concede", "intercede", and "precede".

5. SPELLING PLURAL WORDS

Plural endings are suffixes; therefore, many of the rules about suffixes previously discussed still apply. To form plurals, follow these guidelines:

1. Add "s".

Most words simply add "s" to change their form from the singular (referring to one only) to the plural (referring to more than one).

SINGULAR	PLURAL ENDING	CORRECT SPELLING
bullet	s	bullets
uniform	s	uniforms
vehicle	s	vehicles
window	s	windows

However, if a word ends in "s", "ch", or "sh", or if the plural sound will add another syllable to the pronunciation, then the "es" is used to create the plural form of the word.

SINGULAR	PLURAL ENDING	CORRECT SPELLING
brush	es	brushes
fix	es	fixes
speech	es	speeches
watch	es	watches
witness	es	witnesses

Words ending in "o" may end in "s" or in "es". For example,

SINGULAR	PLURAL ENDING	CORRECT SPELLING
memo	s	memos
piano	s	pianos
hero	es	heroes
potato	es	potatoes

2. Change "f" to "v" and add an "s".

Words ending in "f" or "fe" often change the "f" to a "v" before adding the "s" to form the plural. Look at this change in words such as

SINGULAR	PLURAL
half	halves
leaf	leaves
wife	wives
knife	knives
wharf	wharves

However, "chief" keeps the "f" in its plural form "chiefs", and "roof" has the plural form "roofs".

3. Change "y" to "i" and add "es".

Words ending in "y" in the singular are made plural by changing the "y" to an "i" and adding "es". For example,

SINGULAR	PLURAL
sky	skies
lady	ladies
cemetery	cemeteries

4. Watch for Latin and foreign words.

Some Latin words or foreign words used in English have plural forms that do not follow any particular rule. These plural forms are derived from the plurals used in the ancient or foreign language.

SINGULAR	PLURAL
formula	formulae
gymnasium	gymnasia

oasis	oases
ox	oxen

5. Some words do not change.

Some words do not change whether they are used in the singular or in the plural. For example,

SINGULAR	PLURAL
moose	moose
sheep	sheep

6. Some words change completely.

Some words change completely when they are used in the plural.

SINGULAR	PLURAL
mouse	mice
man	men
goose	geese

If you are unsure of the correct spelling for the plural form of a word, check your dictionary.

6. BRITISH VS. AMERICAN SPELLING

The acceptable spelling of a word might depend on the country in which the word is used. British spelling, which is usually required for legal documents in Canada, differs from American spelling. The British spelling in the list below is derived from the *Concise Oxford Dictionary;* the American spelling is derived from *Webster's New Collegiate Dictionary.*

	BRITISH SPELLING	AMERICAN SPELLING
our/or		
	colour	color
	favour	favor
	honour	honor
	neighbour	neighbor

	odour	odor
	smoulder	smolder
re/er		
	centre	center
	fibre	fiber
	lustre	luster
	metre	meter
	spectre	specter
	theatre	theater
se/ze		
	analyse	analyze
	breathalyser	breathalizer
	paralyse	paralyze
ae/e		
	anaesthesia	anesthesia
	encyclopaedia	encyclopedia
oe/e		
	diarrhoea	diarrhea
	foetus	fetus
	manoeuvre	maneuver
double consonant before endings		
	equalled	equaled
	jewellery	jewelry
	libellous	libelous
	tranquillize	tranquilize
	traveller	traveler
silent "e" before endings		
	abridgement	abridgment
	ageing	aging
	sizeable	sizable
special changes		
	aeroplane	airplane
	carburettor	carburetor
	catalogue	catalog
	cheque	check
	disc	disk
	fulfil	fulfill

grey	gray
programme (except for computers, when it should be program)	program
tyre	tire

Canadian spelling is a blend of British and American spelling. Frequently, spelling choices are determined by the purpose of the work. For example, Canadian legal documents may require British spelling. Spelling choices may also depend on the readers. If a journal article is to be published in the United States, then American spelling would be preferred.

Make sure that the dictionary that you use for reference gives you the appropriate spelling for your writing. For example, do not rely on an American dictionary if you need British spelling. Generally, the Oxford dictionary gives British spelling while the Gage, Random House, or Webster dictionaries give American spelling. In addition, remember that many computer spell check programs frequently use American spelling by default. However, most programs allow you to select which dictionary to use.

7. USING YOUR DICTIONARY

Dictionaries are valuable reference books to guide you to the correct spelling, pronunciation, and use of words. Keep in mind that the few minutes it takes to look up a word could save you from rewriting your work later.

When you purchase your dictionary, take time to get acquainted with it. You will be surprised by how much information it contains. Look at the "Table of Contents" to find the guide to the dictionary. Often, a dictionary includes

1. a guide to understand the syllable breakdown of the words listed;
2. a guide to correct pronunciation, including an explanation of stressed syllables and a phonetic guide;
3. a guide to determine the correct parts of speech for words listed;

4. an etymology key, which explains the origin of words;
5. an explanation of how plurals, comparatives, and irregular forms of the words are spelled.

Some dictionaries also include general information such as metric conversion tables, geographical information, or illustrations of the definitions of words listed. Also, check to see how the definitions of the words in your dictionary are listed. Is the most common definition given first? Is the oldest definition given first?

One of the questions always associated with the dictionary is, "How do you look up a word when you do not know how to spell it?" Here are the steps you can follow to solve that problem:

1. Sound the word out, slowly, so that you can hear the syllables.
2. Think of all the possible ways the word could be spelled.
3. Match the sound of the word you are trying to spell to similar sounds in other words. For example, if you are trying to spell "phlegm", the first letter could be "f" as in "fled", or it could be "p" as in "phone".
4. Scan the entries in the dictionary where you think the word could be located. Using the example "phlegm" again, you will notice that the "g" is silent; however, if you begin by looking up "phlem" and continue to scan the entries, you will find the correct spelling.
5. Check the definition to make sure that you have found the correct word.
6. If all of your efforts fail, ask someone how to spell the word and then verify the spelling in your dictionary. Do not rely on asking someone how to spell the word. You could be given an incorrect spelling.
7. After you have discovered the correct spelling of a word, write it out several times so that you will remember how the word is spelled.

8. COMMONLY MISSPELLED WORDS

The following words are misspelled frequently on police reports.

Note: The words are listed alphabetically across the page.

A

abandon	abdomen	abductor
abet	abortion	absence
absolutely	accelerate	acceptance
access	accessory	accidental
accommodate	accomplice	accosted
accused	acetylene	acknowledge
acquit	acquittal	adjourn
admissible	adolescent	adversary
affidavit	aggravate	aisle
alcohol	alias	alibi
Alzheimer's	amalgamation	ambulance
amended	ammunition	among
amphetamine	analyze	annual
anonymous	antiseptic	aorta
apparatus	apparent	appearance
appellant	apprehended	appropriate
arraignment	arrangement	arrears
arson	artifact	asphyxiate
assailant	assassin	assessment
assistant	asthma	attachment
attest	attorney	audible
autopsy	auxiliary	

B

bail	bailiff	balaclava
ballistics	barbiturate	barrel
barricade	barrister	battalion
bayonet	bazaar	beginning
belligerent	beneficiary	bias
bludgeon	bona fide	boulevard
brassiere	brilliant	bruise
bulletin	burglarize	business
bystander		

C

cadaver	caffeine	calendar
calibre	campaign	cancel
canine	cannabis sativa	capable

cardiac
cartridge
cassette
casualties
category
Caucasian
censor
changeable
chattel
circumstantial
citation
civilian
cocaine
coerce
cognizance
coincidence
collateral
colleague
collusion
comatose
commission
commitment
committee
compel
competent
complainant
complicity
conceive
concurrent
condemn
confidential
confiscate
conjugal
consciousness
consensus
conspicuous
conspirator
constitutional
contagious
contempt
contraband
contraceptive
controversy
conviction
convulsion
coroner
corpse
correspondence
corroborate
counterfeit
courteous
credibility
cremate
culprit
custody
cylinder

D

database
decapitated
deceased
decision
defendant
deferred
delegate
deliberate
delinquent
dependant
dependent
descend
description
detain
detention
deterrent
detonator
development
deviant
deviation
diabetes
diagonal
diarrhea
dilemma
disagreeable
discrepancy
discriminate
dispatcher
disposition
divulge
domicile
dominant
drunkenness
duress
dynamite
dysfunction

E

earnest
efficient
electrocution
elicit
eligible
eliminate
embezzle
eminent
enforceable
entirely
environment
epileptic

equestrian
escalator
evangelist
excessive
exhausted
external
equivalent
espionage
evidence
excite
exhibit
extradited
erratic
ethical
exaggerate
execution
extenuating
extremely

F

facility
fatality
flexible
forehead
formula
fallacy
felon
forceps
foreign
fraudulent
falsify
fictitious
forcible
forensic
fugitive

G

gambling
geriatric
government
grievous
guerilla
gauge
gonorrhea
graffiti
grudge
gymnasium
genuine
gouge
grievance
guarantee

H

habitual
harass
hazardous
homicide
hygiene
hysterical
hallucinate
harbour
heroin
horizontal
hypodermic
handcuff
hazard
homicidal
hostile
hysteria

I

identical
illicit
immigrant
impostor
incapacitate
incessant
inconspicuous
indecent
inevitable
infringement
ideology
illustrate
imminent
inadmissible
incarcerate
incite
incorrigible
indictment
infanticide
ingenious
illegitimate
immediate
impediment
incapable
incendiary
incoherent
incriminate
indispensable
informant
initiate

injunction inoculate insolent
institute insufficient interpreter
interrogate intoxicate investigator
irrelevant irresistible itinerary

J

jamb jealous jeopardy
jewelry judicial jurisdiction

K

khaki kidnap kidnapper
kleptomania knife knowledge

L

laboratory laceration language
larceny legislate legitimate
lenient liability liaison
libellous librarian licentious
lien litigant lucid

M

magazine magistrate maintain
malice malign management
mandatory manila manipulate
manoeuvre marijuana massacre
measurements median mediation
memorandum menace methadone
mileage militia minor
miscarriage miscellaneous misdemeanour
misspelled mitigating moccasin
monotonous moratorium morgue
mortal mortgage mortuary
mucus municipal mutilate
muzzle

N

narcotics necessary negative
negligence negotiate neighbour
neutral nominal notary
notorious nuclear nuisance
nullify

O

obedient
obligation
obscenity
occasion
occult
occupant
occurrence
official
omission
opponent
ordinance
orient
orthodox

P

parachute
paraffin
parallel
paramedic
paraphernalia
pavilion
pedestrian
penitentiary
permissible
persistent
personal
personnel
pertinent
phallic
physician
plaintiff
playwright
polygraph
positive
possession
potential
precede
preliminary
premises
prescription
priority
probable
procedure
proceed
prohibition
projectile
prominent
propeller
prophylactic
prosecute
prosecutor
prostitute
prostitution
protester
psilocybin
psychiatrist
psychopathic
punitive
pursue
pyromaniac

Q

quadrant
quadriplegic
quarantine
quarrel
query
questionnaire
quinine
quotation

R

rabies
racketeer
reasonable
receipt
receding
recidivist
recognizance
recommend
reconcile
reconnaissance
reformatory
refute
reinforcement
relevant
religious
relinquish
remission
rendezvous
repeal
representative
reprieve
rescue
resident
residue
respiration
restaurant
resuscitate

ricochet ritual routine

S

sabotage sacrifice salvage
scenario schedule scheme
schizophrenic seize seniority
sentence separation sequence
sequester sergeant serial
severance sexual sheriff
siege silhouette simultaneous
skeleton sociopath solicit
solicitor soluble specimen
spectator spontaneous strenuous
subpoena suffocate suicide
suppress surrogate surveillance
susceptible suspect suspension
suspicious symmetrical symptom
synagogue syphilis syringe

T

tactical tariff tattoo
taut technique temperament
tendency terrorism testify
testimony thief toboggan
torture tournament tourniquet
trajectory tranquillizer trauma
trespass truancy truly

U

ultimatum umbrella unanimous
uncooperative unlawful unmistakable
urinate useful utility
utilize

V

vacuum vagrancy validate
vandal variance vehicle
vein velocity venereal
vengeance verdict verify
version veterinarian vicious

vigilante	violation	violence
vicinity	viscous	visible
volatile	voluntary	voucher

W

waiver	warrant	weapon
wedge	wholesale	winterize
wiretap	withdrawal	witness
worship	wound	

X

X-ray	Xerox	

Y

yacht	yield	youth

Z

zealot	zinc	zircon

9. CORRECT USE AND SPELLING OF ABBREVIATIONS

Short forms, or abbreviations, may be convenient and space-saving, but they can also confuse a reader who may not recognize the abbreviation. For example, the term MLA may refer to a member of the Legislative Assembly or to the Modern Languages Association. Only use abbreviations if you are sure that their meaning will be clear to your reader.

In formal writing, abbreviations should be avoided. However, when they are used in business or legal documents, abbreviations should be spelled correctly. Abbreviations may be used for the following:

1. Geographical Names

Place names are often abbreviated on forms or on envelopes. There are two standard short forms — the "traditional" short form and the "two letter" abbreviation (preferred by the postal service).

The abbreviations for the Canadian provinces and territories are

PROVINCE OR TERRITORY	TRADITIONAL	TWO LETTER
Alberta	Alta.	AB
British Columbia	B.C.	BC
Manitoba	Man.	MB
New Brunswick	N.B.	NB
Newfoundland and Labrador	Nfld.	NL
Northwest Territories	N.W.T.	NT
Nova Scotia	N.S.	NS
Nunavut	Nun.	NU
Ontario	Ont.	ON
Prince Edward Island	P.E.I.	PE
Quebec	P.Q. (or Que.)	QC
Saskatchewan	Sask.	SK
Yukon Territory	Yuk.	YT

The abbreviations for the states, districts and territories of the United States are

STATE, DISTRICT OR TERRITORY	TRADITIONAL	TWO LETTER
Alabama	Ala.	AL
Alaska	Alaska	AK
Arizona	Ariz.	AZ
Arkansas	Ark.	AR
California	Calif.	CA
Colorado	Colo.	CO
Connecticut	Conn.	CT
Delaware	Del.	DE
District of Columbia	D.C.	DC
Florida	Fla.	FL
Georgia	Ga.	GA
Hawaii	Hawaii	HI

Idaho	Idaho	ID
Illinois	Ill.	IL
Indiana	Ind.	IN
Iowa	Iowa	IA
Kansas	Kans.	KS
Kentucky	Ky.	KY
Louisiana	La.	LA
Maine	Maine	ME
Maryland	Md.	MD
Massachusetts	Mass.	MA
Michigan	Mich.	MI
Minnesota	Minn.	MN
Mississippi	Miss.	MS
Missouri	Mo.	MO
Montana	Mont.	MT
Nebraska	Neb.	NE
Nevada	Nev.	NV
New Hampshire	N.H.	NH
New Jersey	N.J.	NJ
New Mexico	N. Mex.	NM
New York	N.Y.	NY
North Carolina	N.C.	NC
North Dakota	N. Dak.	ND
Ohio	Ohio	OH
Oklahoma	Okla.	OK
Oregon	Oreg.	OR
Pennsylvania	Pa.	PA
Rhode Island	R.I.	RI
South Carolina	S.C.	SC
South Dakota	S. Dak.	SD
Tennessee	Tenn.	TN
Texas	Tex.	TX
Utah	Utah	UT
Vermont	Vt.	VT
Virginia	Va.	VA
Washington	Wash.	WA
West Virginia	W. Va.	WV
Wisconsin	Wis.	WI
Wyoming	Wyo.	WY

2. SI Symbols

In 1971, Canada adopted the Système International d'Unités (SI) metric measurements. SI symbols are not called "abbreviations"; they are called "symbols" and are not followed by periods.

The symbols are always typed in lower case letters, unless they are derived from a person's name, in which case symbols such as "W" (Watt), "Pa" (Pascal), or "N" (Newton) are capitalized. The exception to this practice is the symbol "L" for litre.

SI symbols are not put in italics, nor are they made plural. Common SI symbols include

UNIT OF MEASURE	SYMBOL
degree Celsius	°C
gram	gm
kilogram	kg
kilometre	km
kilopascal	kPa
kilowatt	kW
litre	L
metre	m
millimetre	mm
nautical mile	M
newton	N
square metre	m^2
volt	V

The SI symbols should only be used with numerals. For example,

> The track meet included a 10 km run.
> The substance weighed 2 kg more than expected.

For general references, write the word out in full. For example,

> The ball travelled several metres.
> He weighed a few kilograms more this week.

3. Educational Degrees or Professional Designations

If abbreviations for degrees or professional designations are used, periods follow the initials. If more than one abbreviation is used, they are separated by commas. For example,

Ms. Sally Giomo, B.A., M.A., LL.B., Ph.D.

The title "Dr." should not be used if the degree also designates doctor. For example,

Michael Peters, Ph.D. or Dr. Michael Peters
Michelle Green, M.D. or Dr. Michelle Green

Common abbreviations for degrees and professional designations include

ABBREVIATION	DESIGNATION OR DEGREE
A.C.C.A.	Association of Certified and Corporate Accountants
B.A.	Bachelor of Arts
B.Ed.	Bachelor of Education
B.Sc.	Bachelor of Science
C.A.	Chartered Accountant
D.D.S.	Doctor of Dental Surgery
P. Eng.	Professional Engineer
LL.B.	Bachelor of Laws
M.A.	Master of Arts
M.D.	Doctor of Medicine
Ph.D.	Doctor of Philosophy
R.N.	Registered Nurse
V.S.	Veterinary Surgeon

4. Rank or Titles

The abbreviation for a rank or title should not be used if only the surname is given. For example,

Professor Henderson, Sergeant Hill

However, abbreviations may be used if the full name follows the abbreviation. For example,

Prof. George Henderson, Sgt. Robin Hill

Common abbreviations for military ranks include

RANK	ABBREVIATION
brigadier	Brig.
captain	Capt.
colonel	Col.
commander	Cmdr.
corporal	Cpl.
first lieutenant	1st Lieut.
general	Gen.
major	Maj.
private	Pte.
sergeant	Sgt.

5. Dates

Months and days should only be abbreviated in charts, graphs, or when space is limited. If abbreviations are needed, follow these guidelines:

a) Abbreviate only the months Jan., Feb., Aug., Sept., Oct., Nov., and Dec.
b) Months should not be abbreviated if a specific date is not given. For example,

February was a hectic month.

6. Acronyms

True acronyms are formed by the first letters of the words of the full name. For example,

RCMP — Royal Canadian Mounted Police
NATO — North Atlantic Treaty Organization
SALT — Strategic Arms Limitation Talks
AIDS — Acquired Immune Deficiency Syndrome

Acronyms formed from the first letter of each word are written in capital letters with no periods between the letters. The first time an acronym is used, give the full name followed by the acronym in parentheses which will be used in subsequent references. For example,

> Electrical safety was determined by the Canadian Standards Association (CSA). The CSA is also involved in testing of plumbing products.

Other acronyms are formed from a combination of the first letter and other letters from the words of the name. For example,

> Alcan — Aluminum Company of Canada, Limited
> Nabisco — National Biscuit Company

These acronyms begin with a capital but also include lower case letters.

Acronyms that have become common words are not capitalized. For example,

> radar — radio detection and ranging
> scuba — self-contained underwater breathing apparatus
> laser — light amplification by stimulated emission of radiation

DO NOT use abbreviations for the following:

1. Place names, addresses, days, and months

Unless space is limited, it is preferable to write place names, addresses, days, and months in full.

2. Units of measurement

If the unit of measurement is not preceded by a number, the abbreviation should not be used. For example,

> a cup of sugar, a litre of wine, several yards of rope
> 6 c. sugar, 4 L wine, 9 yd. cloth

3. Titles of courses or subjects of study

Titles of courses or references to subjects of study should not be abbreviated in case the reader is unfamiliar with the names. For example, ENG could refer to engineering or English courses.

Statistics 101, psychology courses

4. Company names

Give company names in full. For example,

Ford Motor Company, Nortel Networks

However, if the company name is referred to for legal purposes, copy it exactly as it appears on company letterhead, including any abbreviations. For example,

Holt, Rinehart & Winston, Sunbeam Corp. (Canada) Ltd.

Remember, too, that the legal names of some companies are different from the names by which those companies are commonly known.

10. NUMBERS: WORDS OR NUMERALS

Generally, numbers that can be expressed in one word are written in words. Therefore, write these numbers out in full:

1. Numbers one through ten

four students, six computers

In formal or legal documents, other numbers may also be written in full. Follow the style established by your department or by the Crown attorney.

2. Round numbers or approximate numbers

a million times, nearly fifty years, approximately six feet tall, several thousand people

3. Time followed by the word "o'clock" or "a.m." or "p.m." may be expressed in words or numerals.

five o'clock, nine o'clock
5 a.m., 9 o'clock

Time expressed using the 24-hour clock should be written using numerals.

18:00, 23:45

4. **If possible, avoid beginning a sentence with a number. However, if it is unavoidable, write the number in full.**

Twenty delegates arrived.

Use numerals for the following references to numbers:

1. **Units of measurement**

2 metres, 8 kilograms

2. **Dates**

May 22, 2002

When the day follows the month, use the numeral alone. When the day precedes the month, use the "th", "rd", or "nd" endings. For example,

March 5, 2002 5th of March, 2002

Dates may also be written using numeric dating. Four digits are used for the year and two are used for each of the month and day.

January 23, 2002 becomes 2002 01 23

3. **Age**

17 years old

4. **Numbers accompanied by abbreviations or symbols**

$65.89, # 3, 19%, 3 a.m., 45 kg

5. **Identification numbers or serial numbers**

Highway 25, Model 354

6. **Room numbers, apartment numbers, street numbers**

Room 67, Apartment 5, 65 Maple Street

If a house number is given for a numbered street, put a hyphen between the house number and the street name. For example,

1789 - 17th Street

11. CAPITAL LETTERS

In general, capitals are used for proper nouns which identify specific people, places, or things. No capitals are used for common nouns which identify general categories, or for general references to people, places, or things.

There are very few instances in which words are typed entirely in capitals. However, words may be placed in capitals in the following items:

1. Legal documents

IN WITNESS THEREOF, the parties . . .

2. Police reports

Peter CROOK sold the stereo to Martin FENCE.

Use capitals for the first letters of the following:

1. Major words in the titles of books, films, plays, poems, songs, broadcasts, and works of art

What's Bred in the Bone (book)
The Grey Fox (movie)
Billy Bishop Goes to War (play)
"Journey to the Interior" (poem)
"Eyes of a Stranger" (song)
Hockey Night in Canada (broadcast)
The West Wind (work of art)

2. Days, months, and holidays

Saturday, July 1, Canada Day

3. Identifying words in addresses

21 Riverside Drive

4. Geographical locations, including the names of nations, provinces, cities, buildings, bridges, parks, mountains, lakes, and rivers

Canada, Nova Scotia, Saskatoon, St. Lawrence Centre, Rainbow Bridge, Jasper National Park, Mount Logan, Lake Huron, Assiniboine River

5. Names of institutions, businesses, organizations, clubs, political parties, and societies

Mount Sinai Hospital, Zenith, Girl Guides of Canada, Rotary Club, Progressive Conservative Party, Humane Society

6. Names of races, tribes, nationalities, and languages

Inuit, Haida, Canadian, French

7. Names of religious orders, faiths and denominations, saints, deities, holy days, fast and feast days, and scriptures

Jesuits, Presbyterian, St. Jude, Buddha, Rosh Hashanah, Feast of St. George, Koran

8. Names of historic periods, events, and documents

The Depression, The October Crisis, Lord Durham's Report

9. Names of sports events and trophies

Olympic Games, Grey Cup

10. Names of flags and emblems

Red Ensign, Stars and Stripes

11. Names of awards, medals, and decorations

Juno Awards, Victoria Cross, Order of Canada

12. Trade names

Kleenex, Xerox, Jell-O

13. Titles of school courses

Psychology 101, Introduction to Literature

14. Terms of rank, or official titles preceding a name or used in place of a specific name, or references to current heads of state

Sergeant Watson, Pope John Paul II, the Duke of Windsor, the Prime Minister, Queen Elizabeth II

15. The terms "royal" or "crown" when referring to governing power or ownership

the Crown, Royal Commission, Crown land, Crown attorney

16. Federal and provincial legislative bodies, and their departments, ministries, agencies, boards, and commissions

House of Commons, Consumer and Corporate Affairs Canada, Ministry of Colleges and Universities, Canada Post, Agriculture Stabilization Board, Canadian Transportation Commission

17. Laws and treaties, and superior court names

War Measures Act, Treaty of Utrecht, Supreme Court of Canada

18. Military forces, military schools, military bases, and political alliances

Canadian Armed Forces, Royal Military College, Base Borden, North Atlantic Treaty Organization

19. Police services, colleges and academies, departments, divisions, and headquarters

Nepean Police Service, Ontario Police College, Identification Unit, 52 Division, Metropolitan Toronto Police Headquarters

Do not use capitals for the items listed below:

1. Compass points when indicating direction

the north corner, south wing, east gallery

However, if the compass direction is part of a name, then a capital is used. For example,

Northern Ireland, North Sea, South America, Pacific Western Airlines

2. Season names when describing times of the year

a warm spring, a colourful autumn

However, if the season name is part of a title or the name of a specific event, then a capital is used. For example,

Annual Spring Report, Winter Madness Sale

3. General references to school subjects

We studied history and politics.

4. Plural references that include common nouns

Names still begin with a capital, but the common nouns are not capitalized.

Mill and Main streets, Humber and Sheridan colleges

5. References to pages, paragraphs, sentences, verses, and lines

page 23, paragraph 5, fifth sentence, third verse, line 213

6. General references to religious sacraments, rituals, and services

a baptism, her prayer, the wedding

7. Proposed or defeated legislation, and working papers

bill C-213, green paper

8. Lower courts and municipal government bodies, and their departments, boards, and commissions

magistrate's court, city council, roads department, school board, cemetery commission

9. Occupational titles and job descriptions

dean, police officer, judge, director of personnel

The terms "former", "acting", and "the late" are not capitalized.

former president of the company, acting manager, the late Mr. Smith

10. General references to military or police rank

an inspector, a general, the sergeant

However, if the reference is to a specific person, then the rank is capitalized. For example,

Inspector Hobbs, General Grant, Sergeant Knight

11. General references to the military or to police departments

the Canadian army, the fraud department

5

Usage

1. CHOOSING THE RIGHT WORD

When you have a large vocabulary, you have more words at your disposal with which to express ideas accurately. With a limited vocabulary, you may find yourself repeating the same words or using them incorrectly as you struggle to make your meaning clear. Furthermore, a limited vocabulary makes it more difficult for you to understand information. For example, if you were told that your witness had been "maligned", would you know whether to protect him, feed him, take him to the hospital, or offer him sympathy?

A large vocabulary strengthens your ability to describe actions or explain ideas precisely. No two words have exactly the same meaning. A person could "disappear" into a crowd or "hide" in a crowd. Both of these words conjure up different images of the person's actions. You do not have to choose large or obscure words to express yourself. You can, however, use the correct and most precise word. A good vocabulary is an asset to everyone who wants to communicate clearly.

There are several simple and effective methods of improving your vocabulary. One of these methods is to read material that you find difficult and that contains unfamiliar words. Find these words in a dictionary, and then re-read the sentences to understand how the words are used. Listen for unfamiliar words in conversations too. If possible, ask the speaker to clarify words that you do not understand, or make a mental note of the unfamiliar words and look them up later. Try to use these words in your writing or in conversation so that you become comfortable with them.

Another method of improving your vocabulary is to play word-oriented games such as *Scrabble*, or word puzzles such as crosswords and cryptograms. Such games give you the opportunity to learn words that are not in common usage.

2. USING A THESAURUS

Writing becomes monotonous when the same word is repeated too often. However, it can be difficult to find a substitute for the over-used word. Fortunately, a thesaurus can guide you to alternative word choices.

In a thesaurus, you will find synonyms (words similar in meaning) and antonyms (words opposite in meaning). The thesaurus can be organized alphabetically or according to general classifications. An alphabetical thesaurus can be used in the same way you would use a dictionary. Words can be found by checking the entries in alphabetical order. In a thesaurus organized by categories, words are found in the "Index" at the back of the thesaurus. The words in the index are listed with entry numbers for the synonyms and antonyms. After finding the entry number, check the entry to find another word that would be appropriate for your use. This type of thesaurus is the most useful if you cannot think of the exact word you want. You can use the category listings given in the "Table of Contents" to direct you to the type of word you should consider.

Word processing programs usually include a software thesaurus. This type of thesaurus can provide alternative choices for a particular word on the screen. The software thesaurus gives you immediate options and allows you to change words quickly. However, the software thesaurus usually fails to give definitions; therefore, you must ensure that the word you choose has the correct meaning in the context of the sentence.

3. WORDS OFTEN MISUSED

To avoid errors, beware of the following "problem" words when you write:

a — use before a consonant, or before "u" or "y"
a street, a uniform, a yacht

an — use before a vowel other than "u", or before a silent "h"
an offence, an apple, an hour

accept — to receive
I accept your recommendation.

except — to exclude
Everyone was invited except Sam.

acclamation — loud support, shouting in someone's honour
The acclamation for the king could be heard for miles.

acclimation — to become accustomed to a new climate or conditions
The acclimation to his new job may take months.

adapt — to modify or change
You must adapt the car to meet the exhaust emission requirements.

adopt — to take as one's own; to take control
The young couple wished to adopt a child.
You should adopt a healthier lifestyle.

advice — (noun) a recommendation
The advice you offered was helpful.

advise — (verb) to caution or warn
The child was advised to ride his bicycle carefully.
Note: "advise" should not be used in place of "inform". "Inform" is a more general term for giving information.

The officer informed the woman that her car had been damaged.

affect (verb) to change or alter, influence
Your foolish act could affect the outcome of this case.

effect (verb) to result in, bring about, create
His careful planning helped to effect a higher budget for this department.
(noun) outcome, result
The effect of this decision will be disastrous.

aggravate to make worse
Verbal abuse could aggravate an emotional situation.

irritate to anger or annoy
Your disrespectful attitude irritates me.

agree to used when referring to a proposal or idea
I agree to this policy change.

agree with used when referring to a person
I agree with your opinion.

aid (noun) assistance
The aid was given to the victim by the ambulance attendant.
(verb) to help, promote, or encourage
Teachers should aid students to study effectively.

aide a person who gives help (usually associated with government)
The Prime Minister's aide distributed the press releases.

AIDS acronym for Acquired Immune Deficiency Syndrome
The fear of AIDS has changed sexual practices.

alibi the fact of having been elsewhere when a crime was committed

The woman's alibi was that she was at her mother's home when her child was attacked.

excuse an explanation

The woman offered a weak excuse for her behaviour.

allot to give by some plan, distribute

The personnel department will allot vacation days according to seniority.

a lot many or much

There have been a lot of complaints about your attitude.

alot not a word (incorrect spelling of "a lot")

allowed to be able to, to be given permission for

The supervisor allowed Marsha to move to a larger office.

aloud out loud

The cadet was asked to read aloud from the notebook.

allude to refer indirectly

The lawyer alluded to the defendant's long involvement in this type of activity.

elude to escape or evade

The convict eluded the search party.

already earlier

You have already failed this course three times.

all ready prepared

We are all ready to go home.

altar (noun) the front table in a church, a place where religious rites are performed

The minister found the altar of the church destroyed.

alter (verb) to change

You cannot alter your testimony.

alternate back and forth, on every other

The cheques will be issued on alternate Fridays.

alternative choice, one of two or more possibilities
Moving to Vancouver appeared to be the only alternative.

among referring to three or more
The estate was divided among the seven children.

between referring to two
We have arranged to divide the driving between the two of us.

amount a quantity
A large amount of heroin was discovered at the airport.

number a quantity that can be counted
A number of cars were left abandoned on this road.

amused entertained
Michael was amused by the joke.

bemused confused, bewildered
Many writers are bemused by computers.

angry upset, enraged
Sergeant Stevens makes the administration angry.

mad insane
It would be mad to declare war.

anyway in any case
I will be blamed anyway.

anyways not a word

appraise to determine value
The furs were appraised by an expert.

apprise to notify
Please keep me apprised of your progress.

bad an adjective describing a person, place, or thing
The bad weather caused problems.

badly an adverb used to describe a verb

He plays the violin badly.

Note: "badly" often is an awkward word to use. In general, avoid the word by rewriting the sentence *(e.g., He does not play the violin well)*.

beside at the side of

The bank is beside the clothing store.

besides (slang) in addition to, moreover

Besides, he is ineligible for parole.

Note: Avoid using "besides" in formal writing.

born having to do with birth

I was born in the summer.

borne having to do with carrying

He has borne the responsibility of leadership for too long.

bridal referring to brides or weddings

Jim was horrified when his girlfriend caught the bridal bouquet at the wedding reception.

bridle part of a horse's harness

The broken bridle disqualified the winner of the equestrian event and had to be investigated.

bullion gold or silver in bar form, or valued by weight

The gold bullion was stolen before it could be minted into coins.

bouillon a thin, clear soup or broth

Chicken bouillon makes a good base for noodle soup.

canvas (noun) a material

Tents are usually made of canvas.

canvass (verb) to survey

We will canvass the neighbourhood to determine public opinion.

censer incense burner

The priest waved the censer during the mass.

censor official with the power to suppress; to make deletions or changes
The censor removed the erotic scenes from the film.

censure expression of disapproval, reprimand
The sergeant was censured by his superiors for his poor conduct.

circumscribe to limit by boundaries, enclose
The fence circumscribed the military base.

circumspect cautious, wary
A circumspect decision instead of a bold initiative may not always be the best course of action.

cite to quote, refer to, or summon to appear in court
A precedent was cited in the defence.

sight (noun) vision; something seen
His sight deteriorated with age.
The mountains were a beautiful sight.

site location
The new site for the athletic building has not been selected.

coarse large or unrefined; rude
The gravel was coarse and unsuitable for a driveway.
Coarse language is offensive.

course route; curriculum
The course was difficult for the rally drivers.
The fingerprinting course was too short.

compare point out the similarities
Compare the first crime scene to the second one.

contrast to point out the differences
In this essay, contrast two different theories of supervisory practices.

complement (verb) to complete or accompany
Choose a tie to complement your suit.

(noun) the number required to fill something

The class had its full complement of students.

compliment expression of praise

I would like to compliment you on your brave action.

connote to imply indirectly, suggest, or allude

The word "customized" connotes personalized and expensive.

denote to indicate directly or show; to symbolize

The green area on the map denotes a park.

conscience a sense of moral standards

His conscience was troubled after he stole the old lady's pension cheque.

conscious to be aware

The victim was conscious but was in a great deal of pain.

console (verb) to soothe and comfort

The minister offered to console the grieving family.

(noun) a bank of switches

The operator at the control console of the nuclear reactor failed to notice the meltdown.

consul official who represents the state and its interests in a foreign country

The consul at the embassy told me to get my passport photograph updated.

contemptible deserving scorn

Intentionally injuring an animal is a contemptible act.

contemptuous disapproving

The old inspector gave the policewoman a contemptuous look.

continual recurring at regular intervals

The ringing of the telephone is continual.

continuous uninterrupted

Continuous rainfall hampered the search.

continuance postponement
The judge granted a continuance in the trial until next Tuesday.

contribute to give a share, donate
Please contribute to the retirement fund.

attribute (verb) to relate to a cause
I attribute this rise in child abuse to economic instability.
(noun) an inherent characteristic
He claimed that conservation of fossil fuels is an attribute of solar energy.

council advisory or administrative body
Martin served on the municipal council for five years.

counsel (noun) advice; legal advisor
The counsel of the Supreme Court is important in lower courts.
The lawyer served as duty counsel.
(verb) to give advice
The priest wanted to counsel the juvenile offender about proper behaviour.

councillor an elected member of a council
Al has served as a town councillor for three years.

counsellor an advisor
Cathy volunteered to be a counsellor at the Rape Crisis Centre.

credible believable
Since he was an eyewitness, his testimony was credible.

creditable praiseworthy, bringing honour or respect
Your creditable conference presentation raises the profile of our entire organization.

delusion alse belief, hallucination
The psychiatric patient suffered from the delusion that he was always being followed.

illusion deceptive appearance
The magician's ability to create the illusion of floating was amazing.

dependant (noun) a person who depends on another for support
His dependants were his wife and three children.

dependent (adjective) relying on something else
The outcome of the trial is dependent on the jury's verdict.

deprecate to express disapproval
He deprecated the thoughtless actions of his son.

depreciate to lessen in value
Gold depreciated after he bought it.

appreciate to increase in value; to be grateful for
Real estate usually appreciates in value.
We would appreciate any assistance you can provide.

diagnosis identification of a disease or condition
After a careful examination of the symptoms, the diagnosis was that the pain was temporary.

prognosis prediction of the course of a disease or condition
The prognosis for his complete recovery was six months.

disinterested impartial, not concerned
The victim cannot present a disinterested account of the crime.

uninterested lacking curiosity or concern
Sarah is uninterested in sewing or cooking.

distinct different, clearly perceptible, unmistakable
The university degree gave Pam a distinct advantage over the other job applicants.

distinctive special, unusual, distinguishing

The distinctive tattoo had an intertwined cherub and serpent.

doubtful unsure

Sergeant Marks is doubtful about your chances of promotion.

dubious a questionable outcome

The success of that plan is dubious.

elicit to evoke, draw forth

I want to elicit a response from you.

illicit illegal

Selling cocaine is an illicit activity.

emigrate to move from a country

They emigrated from England.

immigrate to move to a country

When they left England, they immigrated to Canada.

eminent distinguished, notable, outstanding

Patricia was hailed as an eminent author after her book became a bestseller.

imminent close at hand, about to happen

The darkening sky indicated that a thunderstorm was imminent.

equable steady, even, not easily disturbed

A police officer must have an equable temperament when faced with a dangerous situation.

equitable fair, balanced

The out-of-court settlement was equitable to all of the parties concerned.

every one each one, all

Every one of the suspects was questioned.

everyone everybody

Everyone complains about shift work.

evoke to inspire or draw forth

The comedian is sure to evoke laughter from the audience.

invoke to appeal to law or to a person's authority

The attorney would like to invoke the authority of the judge to call a mistrial.

famous well known

Donald Sutherland is a famous and talented actor.

infamous well known, but in a negative sense

The Boyd gang were infamous bank robbers.

farther to a more distant point

Move the car farther away from the house.

further in addition, more

This problem requires further discussion.

fewer used to refer to numbers

There are fewer than six patrol cars in this area.

less used to refer to amounts

I have less time off than other employees.

flair talent

Beatrice has a flair for painting.

flare (noun) signal flame

The truck driver lit a flare to mark the location of the accident.

(verb) to burst into anger

His temper will flare when he hears that his daughter has been arrested.

flammable easily set on fire

Gasoline is a flammable substance.

inflammable same as flammable (inflammable is preferred in Canada)

non-flammable opposite of flammable

Water is non-flammable.

Note: "Non-inflammable" is not correct.

foregoing previously stated

The foregoing speech was sponsored by the development fund.

forgoing to give up

To lose weight, I am forgoing dessert.

formal ceremonious, or conventional

Graduation ceremonies are formal affairs.

former previous

He was a former student in my class.

forth to proceed ahead

He will go forth with renewed optimism.

fourth number

She is the fourth woman hired for this position.

good describes a person, place, or thing

A good officer should be rewarded.

well describes a verb

He sings well.

good state of health

I am feeling well today.

hanged executed

The prisoner was hanged.

hung suspended

Plants will be hung from the ceiling to make our new offices more attractive.

hear audible, related to the ear

We could hear moans when we entered the house.

here at this place, location

I will meet you here when you finish work.

historic famous or important, referring to past events

The signing of the Magna Carta was an historic event.

historical concerning history

The historical evidence indicates that the battlefield was larger than what is shown on the map.

hyperthermia high fever

Hyperthermia was induced as part of the treatment of the disease.

hypothermia low body temperature

He suffered from hypothermia as a result of falling into the icy water.

imply to suggest

His expensive car and his tailored clothes would imply that he is well paid.

infer to conclude

By examining the budget, we can infer that spending cuts will be drastic.

in regard to with reference to

I am writing in regard to your application.

in regards to incorrect

with regard to referring to

With regard to your résumé, you should elaborate on your previous experience.

interment burial of the dead

Interment of his remains took place at Mount Pleasant Cemetery.

internment confinement

His internment at the prison camp was illegal because he was not given a fair trial.

irregardless not a word

regardless of in spite of

Regardless of the weather, foot patrols must continue.

its used to show ownership or possession

The dog licked its fur.

it's contraction of "it is" or "it has"

It's difficult to stay awake during the midnight shift.

It's been a long night.

judicial referring to the judge or court
The judicial system might be flawed, but it is a necessary part of modern society.

judicious showing good judgment
It is judicious to be pleasant to officials.

laid past form of lay
I laid my equipment on the table yesterday.

lay to set; to produce eggs
I will lay my equipment on the table.
The chicken will lay two eggs a day.

lie repose; untruth
I like to lie down on my bed after work.
You must not lie when you testify in court.

learn to acquire knowledge
He learned about danger when he was assigned downtown.

teach to impart knowledge
Teach your children to avoid strangers.

loose free
If you don't surrender, we will turn the dogs loose.
not tight
The steering felt loose.

lose to misplace
Don't lose your pen.
to suffer defeat
The police golf team never loses the tournament.

material fabric
The material used in the ugly dress was polyester.
matter from which something is made
Material for the book was gathered during years of research.

matériel military equipment and war supplies

The matériel must arrive on time so that the invasion can proceed.

meddle to interfere in someone's affairs
A good mother-in-law should not meddle in her children's marriages.

metal class of elements such as gold, iron, and tin
The army used metal detectors to find mines buried in the ground.

mettle courage, strength of character, stamina
The strenuous fitness programme tested his mettle.

median a line dividing a highway
The car crossed the median when it skidded.

medium (adjective) intermediate
He had a medium build and blonde hair.
(noun) form of communication
Radio is still an important medium.

miner a person who works in a mine
The miner contracted lung disease after breathing coal dust.

minor juvenile, a person under legal age
Billy is still a minor and should not be served alcohol.

moral (noun) a lesson
Fairy tales often contain a moral.
(adjective) righteous
He regarded himself as an upright, moral man.

morale spirit
The morale in this department is very low.

nauseated suffering from an upset stomach, ill
The man complained that he was nauseated and needed some fresh air.

nauseous sickening
The bloody scene was nauseous.

negligence lack of proper care
Driver negligence caused the accident.

negligible too small, trifling, unimportant
The driver's injuries were negligible compared to the serious injuries suffered by the passenger.

notary a notary public, a legal witness
The will was signed by the notary.

notoriety fame
The citation gave her notoriety within the department.

notorious widely but unfavourably known
Billy the Kid was a notorious criminal.

official (adjective) properly authorized
The official symbol of Canada is the maple leaf.
(noun) a person with official duties
The judge is an official of the court.

officious domineering, asserting authority offensively
The officious clerk demanded four pieces of identification.

ordinance religious rite
Peter scrutinized the holy ordinance carefully.
decree
The municipal ordinance stated that garbage pickup would be on Thursdays.

ordnance artillery and military supplies
The military museum included a display of the ordnance used in wars hundreds of years ago.

patience the ability to wait
Patience is still regarded as a virtue, especially in police work.

patients people under a doctor's care

Dr. Darby treated twelve patients before noon.

persecuted to cause to suffer
The bully persecuted the small children in the neighbourhood.
prosecuted involved in a legal action
She has been prosecuted for this type of crime on six other occasions.

personal individual
A choice of career is a personal decision.
personnel employees
Our personnel are highly trained.

precede to go before, go ahead of
Education generally precedes employment.
proceed to go
Proceed to the corner of Mill and Main Streets.

premise a statement assumed to be correct
These conclusions are based on the premise that increased opportunities for advancement will improve motivation.
premises property, land including its building
The suspect entered the premises through the back door.

prescribe to advise use of something
The doctor said he would prescribe exercise, not drugs.
proscribe to forbid, banish, or exile
He wants to proscribe the reading of the book's controversial passages.

prophecy (noun) a prediction of future events
His prophecy of a future earthquake proved to be correct.
prophesy (verb) to foretell events

He tried to prophesy the grades the students would receive at the end of the term.

principal main

The principal concern is money.

amount of money

The principal on the loan doesn't decrease quickly.

head of a school

See the principal, Mr. Macdonald, in the main office of the public school.

principle truth or moral standards

Martha has very high principles.

fundamental law

The law upholds the principle of equality.

quiet to be silent

Please be quiet in the library.

quit to finish, end

The children were told to quit making noise outside of the police station.

quite very much

His sergeant makes him quite angry.

entirely

I'm not quite finished writing this letter.

quote (verb) to repeat a word or phrase from some other source

He always quotes authorities in his essay.

quotation (noun) the word or phrase being quoted

The quotation was obscure and irrelevant.

an estimated price

The contractor gave a quotation of $2,000.

residence a dwelling place, home

I followed the man to his residence.

residents people who live at a specific location

The community relations officer was asked to speak to the residents of the condominium.

respectfully with respect

I respectfully admit that you have more experience.

respectively in the order designated

Make sure that your entries are dated from February to March, respectively.

right to be correct

Your decision is right, but the time is wrong.

direction

Turn right at the dead tree.

entitlement

The suspect has the right to a fair trial.

rite ceremony

Fraternity initiation rites can be funny but dangerous.

sensual related to sex

The striptease was very sensual.

sensuous related to the senses

Perfume has a sensuous appeal.

set to place

I will set this down outside.

sit to be seated

Sit down and explain why your reports are not ready.

stationary fixed, not moving

His car was stationary when it was hit by the other car.

stationery writing paper

You are reminded not to use official stationery for personal letters.

statue piece of sculpture, figurine

The statue in the park has been disfigured.

stature physical size

The man who appeared in the doorway was of an enormous stature.

statute law or regulation

You are expected to enforce the statutes in the Criminal Code.

than a joining word suggesting difference
Michael is taller than Bruce.

then expressing time
I slammed the door, and then I telephoned the police.

their possessive, showing ownership
The family discovered that their computer had been damaged.

there introductory word
There are twelve weapons missing.
indication of place
He attacked me over there.

they're contraction of "they are"
They're making too much noise.

to used as part of a verb
I always have trouble with the verb "to be".
introduces a phrase or word
Give the paperwork to me.

too in addition, also
I wanted to work in the Training Department too.

two the number
Two social workers disagreed with the witness.

tortuous winding, indirect, complicated
The statistical analysis was tortuous and boring.

torturous causing physical or mental pain
The audience behaved as though the opera was torturous.

were part of the verb
We were going to the zoo when we got lost.

we're contraction of "we are"
We're making too much noise.

where	related to location *Where was the riot?*
who	refers to people *He is the man who complained about the fortune teller.*
who's	contraction of "who is" or "who has" *Who's leaving the graffiti in the ladies' room?* *Who's already taken this course?*
whose	showing possession or ownership *Whose car was stolen?*
worse	comparing two items *Marvin is a worse golfer than David.*
worst	comparing three or more items *In fact, Marvin is the worst golfer in our police department.*
yoke	wooden shoulder piece *A yoke was placed over the oxen so that they could pull the wagon.*
yolk	yellow centre of an egg *I was surprised to see a double yolk in the egg.*
your	showing possession or ownership *Your house is in need of repair.*
you're	contraction of "you are" *You're my best friend.*

4. ADDITIONAL USAGE PROBLEMS

Words must be selected carefully so that the reader will not be offended. A reader may be offended when the writer uses words that reflect bias or stereotyping. You should be sensitive to three specific areas of bias: gender, ethnicity, and disability.

(a) Gender Bias

Women now hold positions of power and authority; therefore, the language used to describe such positions should not be male-oriented. Terms such as "chairman", "businessman", "policeman", and "workman" have been replaced by the terms "chairperson", "business person" (or "executive"), "police officer", and "worker".

Pronouns can cause problems when you are trying to eliminate gender bias. While the pronoun "he" is correct for a singular reference, to avoid offending the reader careful writers prefer to change the noun to plural or to eliminate the pronoun. For example:

Grammatically correct:	The supervisor trained his staff effectively.
Less bias: (noun changed to plural)	Supervisors train their staff effectively.
Less bias: (pronoun eliminated)	The supervisor trained the staff effectively.

In order to keep your writing gender-free, follow these guidelines:

1. Parallel Treatment

Ensure that men and women are described in equal terms. For example, "man and wife" is not a parallel expression. Instead, use "husband and wife". "Ladies and men" is not a parallel phrase. Use "ladies and gentlemen" instead.

2. Job Titles

Avoid adding "lady", "female", or "woman" to descriptions of occupations (*e.g.*, "lady lawyer", "female doctor", or "career woman"). Descriptions of job titles should be inclusive terms that are appropriate for both men and women, such as "firefighter", "police officer", "executive manager", or "sales clerk".

3. "Girl" and "Man"

The word "girl" should be avoided because it sounds patronizing and is a term that excludes men. For example, change "office girl" to "office worker", "dancing girl" to "dancer", "college girl" to "college student", and "calendar girl" to "calendar model". Often, women are described as "girls" rather than by their job titles. Do not refer to a secretary as a "girl", and do not refer to a group of secretaries as "the girls".

The word "man" should be avoided because it excludes women. For example, change "craftsman" to "artisan", "workman" to "worker", "family man" to "homebody", "hit man" to "assassin" or "killer", and "mankind" to "humanity".

4. Feminine Endings

Words used to describe women do not require feminine endings.

For example, instead of "directress", "authoress", "murderess", "seductress", and "executrix", use "director", "author", "murderer", "seducer", and "executor".

5. Salutations

It is inappropriate to begin a letter "Dear Sir" when the recipient may be a woman. Using "Dear Sir or Madam" is not parallel language since women are rarely called "Madam". An inclusive form of address, such as "Dear Manager" or "Dear Resident" is preferred.

Use the term "Ms." as a parallel term to "Mr.", unless the woman states a preference for the title "Miss" or "Mrs." Do not assume that a wife has the same last name as her husband. Remember former Prime Minister Joe Clark and his wife Maureen McTeer? In this case, use Ms. Maureen McTeer, not Ms. Maureen Clark or Mrs. Joe Clark.

6. He/She

The singular pronoun "he" can be avoided in three ways:

a) Change the noun to plural. For example, "Police officers need their notebooks."
b) Talk directly to the reader by using "you". For example, "You need your notebooks."
c) Replace the pronoun with an article. For example, "Police officers need a notebook."

The "he/she" construction should be used sparingly.

(b) Ethnicity

Writing must not display bias according to nationality, race, colour, or culture. For example, when writing about a Canadian citizen, do not assume that the Canadian is of a particular race, colour, or culture. Citizenship is not an indicator of ethnic group or race.

The terms "anglophone" and "francophone" refer to language use, not to ethnic origins or provincial residence. The term "First Nations" includes the Inuit nations, the Indian nations, and the Métis. However, further identification would be made by referring to the person's tribe or nation, such as "Huron", "Cree", or "Caribou".

(c) Disability

Biased language focuses attention on a person's disability, while preferred language focuses on the person. The phrase "a disabled person" points to the disability before it refers to the person. It is preferable to use the phrase "a person with a disability." It is even better to identify the specific disability by using a phrase such as "employees who are visually impaired" or "students with special learning needs."

Avoid referring to a person as "the diabetic" or "the epileptic". In addition, note that paralysis and deafness are conditions and not diseases. People who are unable to speak are "mute", not "dumb", and people who have "Down's syndrome" should not be described as "Mongoloid".

Other preferred terms include

walks with crutches	NOT	needs crutches
seizure	NOT	fit
uses a wheelchair	NOT	needs a wheelchair
person with mental illness	NOT	mentally ill person

The elimination of bias in writing should not be seen as superficial. Instead, bias should be eliminated to reflect contemporary standards and attitudes. As standards and attitudes continue to change, language use must also evolve to reflect those changes.

6

Punctuation

Punctuation helps the reader recognize the proper phrasing in a sentence. To write well, it is important to know all of the punctuation marks and how to use them correctly.

1. COMMAS

The comma is the most abused punctuation mark. Some writers are so terrified of the comma that they simply pretend that it does not exist. Other writers liberally sprinkle their writing with commas, hoping that a few of them will fall in the right places. At some time, every student of writing has heard the advice "Put the comma where you take a breath." This advice is not very reliable. If this rule were followed, the placement of commas would vary depending on the writer's lung capacity! Fortunately, you do not have to depend on panting and wheezing to determine the placement of commas.

Commas are used in the following ways:

1. **Commas are used to separate a series of three or more words or phrases in a sentence.**

> The bank robbers used electronic silencing devices, laser cutters, rope, and dynamite.

The comma before the "and" in the series is optional.

We looked on the beach, in the ravine and along the railway tracks.

However, the comma should be added before the "and" in the list if there is the possibility that the last two items in the series could be misread or misunderstood.

We had potatoes, lettuce, pork, and beans.

In this example, if the comma is not used before the "and", the reader may not know whether the sentence refers to roast "pork" and green "beans" or to canned "pork and beans". Include the comma before the final "and" if the last two items could be misread as one item.

If the sentence refers to only two items, no comma is used.

He blamed his downfall on gambling and liquor.

2. Commas are used in a series of descriptive words (known as "adjectives" or "adverbs").

He was intelligent, responsible, and dull.
Sylvia drove quickly, carelessly, and dangerously.

The comma replaces the word "and" in a series; if the word "and" is repeated, the sentence could become monotonous. However, if you cannot substitute "and" for the comma in a series, omit the comma.

A tall (and) beautiful (and) blonde woman waited in the lobby.
A tall, beautiful, blonde woman waited in the lobby.

Notice there is no comma between "blonde" and "woman".

3. A comma is used after a name or an introductory direct address.

Name:

Constable Swithens, you are a bumbling fool.

Note: Don't use a comma if the name is not part of a form of address.

Constable Swithens is a bumbling fool.

Introductory Phrase:

Ladies and gentlemen, please welcome our guest speaker.

4. When phrases from the end of the sentence are moved to the beginning, a comma is placed after the phrase.

The jury was sequestered until the trial was over.
(phrase at end — no comma)

Until the trial was over, the jury was sequestered.
(comma after the introductory phrase)

5. A comma is used after "Yes" or "No" at the beginning of a sentence.

Yes, I attend university.
No, she shouldn't be given a cigarette.

6. If two sentences (which can also be called "independent clauses") are joined by conjunctions such as *and, but, for, nor, or, so,* or *yet,* a comma is used before these conjunctions. Note: Remember these conjunctions by using the acronym "fan-boys" — f(for) a(and) n(nor) b(but) o(or) y(yet) s(so).

The road conditions were bad, and there were numerous accidents.
The officer arrived at the scene of the robbery, but she was unable to catch the suspect.

Remember, two sentences cannot be joined with a comma. This creates a "comma splice" which is a type of run-on sentence.

Comma Splice:

The car was stopped at the border, it was searched for narcotics.

Correct:

The car was stopped at the border. It was searched for narcotics.

7. A comma is used after the salutation in an informal letter.

Dear Mom,

8. A comma is used to separate numbers or words with adjacent numbers that could be misread.

In 2001, 12 homicides were investigated.
In April, 25 robberies were committed.
Of the people over the age of 65, 20 percent live in poverty.

9. A comma is used in addresses and place names.

The suspect was seen in Winnipeg, Manitoba, on July 16, 2002.

Do not use a comma if only one element of the place (city or province) or date (one year, or only the month and date) is given.

He lived in Thunder Bay before his retirement.
The case was heard in 2001.
The drugs are scheduled to arrive on October 12.

10. A comma is used to separate a direct quotation from introductory words like "he said".

Notice the placement of the commas in the following examples:

The man said, "I know where they are hiding."
"I know where they are hiding," the man said.

Do not use a comma if a question mark or exclamation point is part of the quotation and precedes the descriptive words.

"Where are you going?" she asked.

If the quotation comes after the descriptive words, the comma is retained before the quotation marks.

She asked, "Where are you going?"

No comma is used with indirect quotations.

He asked if the injured dog had been taken to the veterinary hospital.

11. Commas are used to surround words or phrases that are not essential to the meaning of the sentence.

These words and phrases generally fall into three categories: "appositives", "non-restrictive phrases", and "parenthetical expressions". These terms identify descriptive words and phrases that could be omitted from the sentence.

Appositives (or identifying words and phrases):

I warned the family not to allow Foxy, the dog, to continue barking.

Notice that "the dog" could be removed from the sentence without altering significantly the meaning of the sentence.

I warned the family not to allow Foxy to continue barking.

Non-restrictive Phrase and Clauses (or descriptive groups of words):

If a descriptive phrase could be removed from the sentence without changing its meaning, place commas around the phrase.

Constable Fitzpatrick, who works in the Training Department, organized the seminar.

The main idea of the sentence remains if the phrase is removed.

Constable Fitzpatrick organized the seminar.

No commas are used around a group of words that form a "restrictive phrase" (a phrase essential to the meaning of the sentence).

All police officers who speed unnecessarily will be reprimanded.

Eliminating the phrase "who speed unnecessarily" changes the meaning of the sentence.

All police officers will be reprimanded.

Parenthetical Expressions (or words or expressions added as asides):

Words like "however", "moreover", "nevertheless", "therefore", "consequently" or expressions like "I think", "he hopes" are used to give sentences a conversational or informal tone or to enhance coherence. These words are set off with commas because, like the other expressions just discussed, they can be eliminated from the sentence without changing its meaning.

He was, however, last on the list of award winners.
His tone of voice, I think, was insulting.

2. SEMICOLONS

The use of the semicolon is reflected in its appearance. It is a combination of a comma and a period. It is considered to be stronger than a comma but weaker than a period. Semicolons are used in the following ways:

1. **A semicolon joins two related sentences.**

    Teenagers often become bored during summer vacation; vandalism could result from this boredom.

2. **If two sentences are joined by a transitional word like "however", "moreover", "nevertheless", "then", or "therefore", a semicolon is placed before the joining word and a comma is placed after it.**

    The boy had been missing for several days; however, he was found unharmed.

3. **Semicolons are used in a series of items already containing commas to co-ordinate groups of items within the series.**

    We invited Peter, the new constable, David, the investigator, and Dennis, the psychologist, to be on the panel.

    There could be three people on the panel, or there could be five depending on how the items in the series are grouped. Is Peter a new constable? Are they two different people, one referred to by name and the other by occupation? To make it clear that the first two entries refer to the same person, use a semicolon to show the relationship.

> We invited Peter, the new constable; David, the investigator; and Dennis, the psychologist; to be on the panel.

3. PERIODS

The period (or "full stop" or "end stop") is one of the most common punctuation marks. The period is used in the following ways:

1. A period is used at the end of a sentence.

Three kinds of sentences end in periods.

Statements (or Declarative Sentences):

> The mechanic couldn't fix the car.

Commands (or Imperative Sentences):

> Place your fingertips on the ink-pad.

Indirect Questions

> He asked if a syringe could be purchased.

2. A period is used to show numerical divisions.

> Decimals — 4.2 accidents per month
> Money — $8.52

3. A period is used after most abbreviations.

David Anderson, B.A., LL.B.
He brought books, pencils, pens, etc., to class.
Mrs. Jennifer Parker
Ms. Carol Myers
Mr. John Frye
a.m. and p.m.

Periods are not used after

a) Call letters for radio or television stations

CBC, CFNY, WBQB, WRNR

b) Commonly used short forms

gym, math, memo

c) Acronyms for organizations or agencies

UN, YMCA, RCMP, FBI

However, if the agency uses periods in the name, follow the established style. For example, O.P.P. for Ontario Provincial Police.

d) the title "Miss"

Miss Amanda Jones

4. A series of three periods (called an "ellipsis") is used to show omission of words.

This is a useful device in research papers when you want to use part of a quotation. For example, the full quotation could read:

"Our studies have shown that many students who decide to become police officers in their early years of high school change their minds before they graduate."

You could eliminate some of the words by using an ellipsis.

"Our studies have shown that many students who decide to become police officers . . . change their minds . . . ".

Notice that four periods are located at the end of the quotation. Three periods are the ellipsis, and the fourth period after the quotation marks denotes the end of the sentence. When using an ellipsis, it is important to keep the correct grammatical structure of the sentence, and to avoid altering the meaning or intent of the original sentence.

4. COLONS

A colon is used as an introduction or to separate items. A colon is used in the following ways:

1. **A colon is used to introduce a list that is introduced by a phrase such as "the following" or "as follows".**

   A good deputy chief should possess the following traits: honesty, patience, strength, and courage.

2. **A colon is used to separate the place of publication from the publisher in a book listing.**

   Toronto: Carswell

3. **A colon is used after the salutation in certain forms of formal business letters, unless the system called "open punctuation" is used.**

   Dear Chief Atkins:
   Dear Committee Members:

4. **A colon is used in Biblical references.**

   Genesis 1:2-5

5. **A colon is used to separate hours and minutes.**

   8:56 a.m.

6. **Colons often separate a title from a subtitle.**

   Shift Work: A sociological perspective

5. QUESTION MARKS AND EXCLAMATION POINTS

Question marks and exclamation points are used in the following ways:

1. A question mark is used at the end of a direct question.

Do you believe that your civil rights were violated?

Question marks are not used at the end of indirect questions.

He asked if he could speak to his lawyer.

2. An exclamation point is used to end an emphatic or extremely forceful statement.

Look out!
Stop or I'll shoot!

It is not correct to use multiple exclamation points. Also, the exclamation point is not used in formal business writing.

6. DASHES

A dash is used to mark a sudden break in thought or to set off an added explanation more emphatically than by using commas. A dash is used in the following ways:

1. A dash is used to mark a sudden break in thought.

I think he was tall — no, he was shorter than Lenny.

2. A dash is used to emphasize an identifying word or phrase.

He was arrested for a serious crime — first degree murder.
The people — judge, attorney, and jury — are important to the legal system.

Note: When writing with a typewriter or word processor, a dash is made with two hyphens.

7. SLASHES

Avoid using the slash in formal writing. A slash is used in the following way:

1. In informal writing, a slash is used between terms to indicate that either word is applicable.

Time/money management is essential.
The system runs with fax and/or modem.

2. The slash is used to avoid gender identification.

The officer must sign his/her notebook.
He/she will provide proper authorization.

Note: The use of "he/she" or "his/her" makes writing awkward. It is preferable to change the noun to the plural so that the pronoun "they" can be used.

Officers must sign their notebooks.
They will provide proper authorization.

The slash is also used as a substitute for the word "per" in ratio expressions.

He was driving at 100 km/h.

The reverse slash "\" is not used in writing; however, it often forms part of computer addresses.

8. HYPHENS

Hyphens are used to express the idea of a unit and to avoid ambiguity. Hyphens are used in the following ways:

1. Use a hyphen to join compound words.

mother-in-law, Attorney-General, self-control

Note: Words that are spelled with hyphens will have the hyphens indicated in the dictionary.

2. Hyphens join words used as a single adjective before a noun.

The well-known fugitive was captured.

Note: A hyphen is not used when the compound adjective follows the noun or when the first word is an adverb ending in "ly".

The captured fugitive was well known.
The brilliantly executed plan saved many lives.

3. A hyphen is used with numbers from 21 to 99 or with fractions that are written out in full.

seventy-five
ninety-seven
two-thirds

Compound adjectives containing numbers are also hyphenated. For example,

ten-year-old
two-storey
forty-hour

4. Hyphens are used to show that words are being spelled out.

He said his name was spelled G-r-e-i-g not G-r-e-g.

5. A hyphen is used to split a word at the end of a line.

Big Bob, who specializes in identification, was a para-
trooper in the army before he joined the police service.

Remember to break the word after a syllable. (You can check how the word is broken into syllables by looking it up in the dictionary.) Notice that the hyphen goes at the end of the line, not at the beginning of the next line. If possible, avoid using the hyphen to break words. Instead, move the entire word to the next line. If text is computer typeset (for instance, this book), the margins are justified and the computer program uses its own style for breaking words. This may not necessarily follow dictionary rules of syllable division.

6. A hyphen is used with the prefixes "ex", "self", "half", "quarter", and with the suffix "elect".

ex-convict, self-motivated, half-truth, quarter-interest, president-elect

The prefix "semi" is always hyphenated when the next word begins with "a".

semi-annual, semi-automatic

Other words may or may not be hyphenated with the prefix "semi". If you are not sure, check your dictionary.

semicircle, semi-detached, semi-skilled

7. A hyphen is used when joining a single capital letter to a word.

U-turn, H-bomb, S-curve, T-bone

8. A hyphen is used to connect dates except when they are preceded by "from" or "between".

the 1989-91 annual reports are filed in the library.
The deficits covered the period from April to June.

9. PARENTHESES AND BRACKETS

These are parentheses: ( )
These are brackets: [ ]

Parentheses and brackets are used in the following ways:

Parentheses

1. Parentheses are used to set off additional information or references.

The position of the body was noted before the ambulance arrived (see Chart 1).
The first call (at 06:00) was not classified as a suicide threat.

2. **Parentheses are used to set off the number or letter that identifies the item in a list.**

    The chapter outlined (a) the procedure, (b) the dangers, and (c) the consequences.

3. **Parentheses are used to enclose information, usually numbers, to ensure accuracy.**

    You owe the bank sixty-five dollars ($65.00).
    He exceeded the speed limit by twenty-five kilometres (25 km).

Brackets

1. **Brackets are used to add clarifying information, omitted words, or editorial comments to a quotation.**

    The report [#52716] has been misplaced.
    The robber's note stated, "Give [me] all your money."

2. **Brackets are used to enclose the word "sic" showing that a quotation contained errors, usually misspellings, in the original.**

    The "sic" indicates that the error has been copied directly from the original source.

    The killer left the message "Hilp [sic] me" on the wall in the garage.

10. QUOTATION MARKS

Quotation marks are either single or double types. Unless otherwise indicated below, double quotation marks are used. Quotation marks are used in the following ways:

1. **Quotation marks are used to enclose the exact words spoken by a person (a direct quotation).**

    Michael replied, "I'm innocent."
    "I'm innocent," Michael replied.
    "I'm a good boy," Michael claimed, "and I'm innocent."

2. **Quotation marks are used to enclose a short passage of text from a source.**

   In *Teenage: the Misunderstood Age,* he writes, "Even with the bounds of parental authority firmly established, teens may become confused about morality."

3. **Quotation marks are used to enclose definitions.**

   The dictionary defines a line as "the shortest distance between two points."

4. **Quotation marks are used to enclose words being referred to as words or used for a special purpose such as slang.**

   Don't overuse "proceeded" in your reports.
   Do you remember when "groovy" and "out of sight" were popular expressions?

5. **Quotation marks are used to enclose the titles of short poems, songs, articles, short stories, and chapters.**

   The children sang "99 Bottles of Beer."
   Please read "Computers and the Police" in *On the Beat* magazine.

6. **Single quotation marks have only one use. Single quotation marks are used to punctuate a quotation within a quotation.**

   The neighbour explained, "When I arrived I heard his wife yell, 'Get away from me'."

11. ITALICS

Italics can only be produced with a typewriter or printer with italic typeface. If italic typeface is not available, underlining should be used. The following items should be placed in italics (or underlined if italic typeface is not available):

1. **Titles of publications (including the names of books, newspapers, and magazines)**

   Understanding Criminal Offenses, The Globe and Mail, Canadian Encyclopedia, FBI Bulletin, Police Chief, RCMP Gazette

2. **Dramatic productions (including the names of television shows, radio shows, plays, films, operas, and ballets)**

   60 Minutes, WRNR Solid Gold, Hamlet, The Lord of the Rings, Carmen, The Nutcracker Suite

3. **Artistic works (including the names of paintings and sculptures)**

   West Wind, The Archer

4. **Names of specific vehicles (including the names of ships, trains, and airplanes)**

   Bluenose, Orient Express, Spirit of St. Louis

5. **Foreign words and phrases that are not commonly used in English**

   tour de force, ex curia, prima facie, circa, Zeitgeist

6. **Legal citations (including references to cases and statutes)**

   Smith v. Jones, Trade-marks Act

12. APOSTROPHES

Apostrophes are used in the following ways:

1. **Use an apostrophe to show possession (or ownership).**

   Since it is awkward to use "the bike of the boy" or "the rings of the ladies", the phrases are shortened to "the boy's bike" and "the ladies' rings" and the possession is indicated by the use of an apostrophe. The basic rule for determining where to put the apostrophe is:

   If the word does not end in "s", add an apostrophe and "s".
   If the word ends in "s", just add an apostrophe.

For example,

WORDS NOT ENDING IN "S"	WORDS ENDING IN "S"
lady's ring	students' pub
boy's shirt	dogs' kennels
suspect's appearance	boxes' labels
men's room	books' covers
yesterday's hero	toys' pieces

Note: The apostrophe is not used to form the plural of words, for example, one lady — two ladies, one man — two men, one book — many books, one child — several children.

Some possessives are more difficult to indicate. Follow these guidelines:

a) To show joint possession, put the apostrophe and "s" on the last word only.

   Susan and Mark's boat

b) To show separate possession, put the apostrophe and "s" on both words.

   the mayor's and the police chief's problems

c) For hyphenated words, put the apostrophe and "s" on the last word only.

   my mother-in-law's house
   the commander-in-chief's speech

d) For company names, follow the form used by the company.

   Maclean's magazine, General Motors dealership

e) For geographical names, follow the form used in the atlas.

   Devil's Island, Clarks Harbour

2. An apostrophe is used in a contraction to show omission of letters.

could not — couldn't
cannot — can't

he is — he's
rock and roll — rock'n'roll
it was — 'twas
until — 'til

These contractions are used to give writing an informal, chatty or poetic tone. However, contractions are rarely used in business, academic, or legal writing where a formal tone must be maintained.

3. Apostrophes are not used with possessive pronouns.

The pronouns "my", "mine", "your", "ours", "his", "her", "hers", "its", "our", "ours", "their", "theirs" and "whose" are already possessive and do not need an apostrophe.

my car, your badge, his coat, its fur, our computer, whose funeral

The possessive pronouns are often confused with the following contractions:

you're — you are
it's — it is
they're — they are
there's — there is
who's — who is

The contraction that causes the most usage problems involves the word "it".

its — a possessive pronoun (already possessive, like "his" or "hers")

The car had its tires slashed.

it's — the contraction for "it is"

It's a busy night.

Use this guide and you'll avoid countless errors:

Never write "it's" without saying to yourself "it is". Never read "it's" without reading "it is".

7

Sentence Structure

Imagine reading a passage written without the benefit of sentences.

> our research into this problem yielded very little witnesses were interviewed but their accounts varied substantially review your notes and let me know if there are any other sources that we can use to continue our investigation

When sentences are used, the writing is easier to read and to understand.

> Our research into this problem yielded very little. Witnesses were interviewed, but their accounts varied substantially. Review your notes and let me know if there are any other sources that we can use to continue our investigation.

Correct sentence structure is necessary for the clear expression of ideas. In order to strengthen sentences, you must understand how sentences work. Just as you would not attempt to repair a car engine without knowing the difference between a fan belt and a distributor cap, you should not attempt to fix sentence problems without knowing the differences between various parts of speech.

1. PARTS OF SPEECH

Parts of speech are determined by the functions that words perform within sentences. There are eight different parts of speech.

(a) Nouns

Nouns name a person, place, thing, idea, quality, or emotion. Nouns can be either singular (referring to one), or plural (referring to more than one).

Person or people:
actor, boxers, child, Harvey, Samantha, writers, Captain Kirk
Place or places:
Wasaga Beach, Tokyo, cities, offices, jail
Thing or things:
dog, lice, television, book, desk, cosmetics
Idea or ideas:
patriotism, communism, revenge, liberty
Quality or qualities:
beauty, truth, equality, faith
Emotion or emotions:
love, hate, passions, sadness, pity

(b) Pronouns

Pronouns are a substitute for nouns in a sentence and are used in order to avoid repeating nouns. "I", "you", "he", "she", "it", "we" and "they" are all pronouns. There are different types of pronouns, including

PRONOUN TYPE	EXAMPLE
Possessive	mine, your, yours, our, ours, his, hers, its, their, theirs
Reflexive	myself, yourself, himself, herself, itself, themselves.

(c) Adjectives

Adjectives describe nouns. There are several different types of adjectives, including

ADJECTIVE TYPE	EXAMPLE
Articles	a, an, the
Comparative	hard, harder, hardest
Descriptive	beautiful, tall, eerie, bashful
Demonstrative	this, these, those
Interrogative	what, whose, which
Numerical	one, two, five, twelve

(d) Verbs

Verbs give information about the subject of the sentence by describing an action or state of being. For example,

Action:
moved, fell, thrust, jog, burn, felt, cried
State of being:
is, are, was, were

Verbs describe action in relation to time by using past, present, or future tenses.

Past tense:
I walked
Present tense:
I walk
Future tense:
I will walk

Verbs can be used in either the active or passive voice. If the subject performs the action, then the verb is active. If the subject receives the action, then the verb is passive. For example,

Brenda kicked the constable. (active verb)
The constable was kicked by Brenda. (passive verb)

(e) Adverbs

Adverbs describe verbs, adjectives, or other adverbs. Often, adverbs indicate time (immediately, later), or place (there, here). They also qualify (very, quite, thoroughly), or describe "how" (carefully, arrogantly, quickly). Many adverbs end in "ly".

(f) Prepositions

Prepositions introduce phrases. Common prepositions include: about, above, after, against, along, among, around, at, before, behind, below, beneath, beside, between, beyond, by, concerning, down, during, except, for, from, in, inside, into, like, near, of, off, on, over, past, through, throughout, to, toward, under, until, up, upon, with, within, without.

(g) Conjunctions

Conjunctions are used to join one idea to another. There are several types of conjunctions, including:

CONJUNCTION TYPE	EXAMPLE
Co-ordinate	for, and, nor, but, or, yet, so
Subordinate	after, during, if, when
Correlative	both . . . and, either . . . or, neither . . . nor
Conjunctive adverbs	also, consequently, however, moreover, then, therefore

(h) Interjections

Interjections are words used to express emotion or surprise, and they are often followed by an exclamation mark. Interjections include: "ah", "alas", "great", "help", "hey", "hooray", "no", "oh", "ouch", "ugh", "yuck", and "wow". Interjections are rarely used in formal writing.

2. HOW TO RECOGNIZE COMPLETE SENTENCES

A sentence is more than a thought written with a capital letter at the beginning and a period at the end. Grammatically, a sentence must be a complete thought expressed with a subject and a verb. In order to recognize a complete sentence, you must be able to recognize the subject and the verb.

(a) The Subject of the Sentence

The subject of the sentence identifies who or what you are writing about in the sentence. The subject will always be either a noun (a word for a person, place, or a thing), or a pronoun (I, you, he, she, it, we, they).

Sometimes a sentence will have only one subject.

The accused was fingerprinted.

The sentence is about "the accused". "Accused" is a noun and is the subject of the sentence. However, a sentence may have more than one subject.

Smith and King investigated the assault charges.

The sentence is about both "Smith" and "King". Both of these nouns are subjects of the sentence. A subject consisting of two or more nouns is called a "compound subject".

Subjects would be easy to identify if all sentences were short and simple; however, writers do not always use short and simple sentences. For example, find the subject in the following sentence:

After the explosion in the parking lot near the airport, an ambulance was dispatched.

To identify the subject in this sentence, it is helpful to know that the subject of a sentence will not be in a phrase which begins with a preposition (called a "prepositional phrase"). Eliminating the prepositional phrases in this sentence will leave only a few words from which to choose the subject:

(After the explosion) (in the parking lot) (near the airport), an ambulance was dispatched.

"Ambulance" is the subject of the sentence and is a noun.

Although a sentence must contain a subject, in the case of a command (also called an "imperative sentence"), the subject is always understood to be the pronoun "you", even though "you" may not appear in the sentence. A command is always given directly to a person, but it is awkward to say or write

You stop!

As a result of this, the "you" is dropped and the sentence becomes

Stop!

Yet, the subject is understood to be "you".

(b) The Verb

The verb in a sentence expresses the action or state of being of the subject of the sentence. For example,

The robber shot the store owner. (action)
Constable Waite is a hero. (state of being)

In general, verbs are words that express action such as "run", "hit", "shoot", "walk", or "chase".

Verbs that express a state of being are commonly used as linking, or "auxiliary", verbs. For example,

The officer is brilliant.
Joe appeared interested.
The weather became stormy.
Your report seems fine.
This looks repulsive.
He felt depressed.

These verbs link the subject to the information that follows the verb. This information about the subject is called the "subjective complement".

Verbs are also described as being "transitive" or "intransitive". Transitive verbs require a direct object to complete the meaning of the verb. Direct objects complete the verb by answering the questions "who" or "what". For example,

The suspect opened the door.
Have you seen the sergeant?

Intransitive verbs do not require direct objects to complete their meaning. These verbs can "stand alone". For example,

The victim died.
Steve left.

Verbs change their forms according to person and number (first, second, or third person, and singular and plural), tense (past, present, or future), voice (active or passive), and mood (indicative, imperative, or subjunctive). This makes verbs flexible, but it also makes them the most difficult parts of speech to use correctly.

(i) Person and number

Verbs change their form according to person. For example,

First person:
I walk.
Second person:
You walk.
Third person:
He walks.

Verbs also change according to number. If the subject of the sentence is singular, the verb must be singular. If the subject of the sentence is plural, the verb must be plural. For example,

Singular:
The car is in the parking lot.
Plural:
The cars are abandoned.

For more information on matching the verb to the subject, see the section on Agreement below in this chapter.

(ii) *Tense*

Verbs change in form to indicate time. The three main tenses in English are past tense, present tense, and future tense. These three forms are also called "simple tenses".

Past tense:
The victim identified the accused.
Present tense:
The victim identifies the accused.
Future tense:
The victim will identify the accused.

To form the other tenses of verbs, you must know the principal parts of a verb. These parts are the present tense, the past tense, and the past participle. By the way in which these parts are formed, the verbs are known as "regular verbs" or "irregular verbs".

Regular verbs form their past tense and past participle by adding "d" or "ed" to the present tense form of the verb. For example,

PRESENT TENSE	PAST TENSE	PAST PARTICIPLE
hope	hoped	hoped
stop	stopped	stopped
cry	cried	cried

Notice that, in some cases, the spelling of the present form may be changed slightly to form the past tense and the past participle.

Irregular verbs form their past tense and past participle in non-standard ways. For example,

PRESENT TENSE	PAST TENSE	PAST PARTICIPLE
swim	swam	swum
beat	beat	beaten
set	set	set

Most dictionaries provide the forms of irregular verbs.

When some of the tenses are expressed, the verb may include an auxiliary verb. Auxiliary verbs include "be", "have", "do", "would", "should", and "could". In other cases, the main verb may be the present participle, which is the present tense verb with "ing" added.

In simple tense forms, the time is expressed by the main verb. For example,

I sang. (past tense)
The sergeant sings well. (present tense)
Billy will sing at the concert. (future tense)

In perfect tense, time is expressed by the auxiliary verb. For example,

I had asked for more computers. (past perfect tense)
The delegates have asked for coffee. (present perfect tense)
We will have asked for assistance three times. (future perfect tense)

Simple and perfect tenses can also be expressed as progressive verb forms, which consist of the correct form of the verb "to be" with the present participle. For example,

TENSE	EXAMPLE
past	was asking, was seeing
present	is asking, is seeing
future	will be asking, will be seeing
past perfect	had been asking, had been seeing
present perfect	has been asking, has been seeing
future perfect	will have been asking, will have been seeing

(*iii*) *Voice*

Verbs may be expressed by using either active or passive voice. In active voice, the subject of the sentence performs the action. For example,

The officer arrested the student.
The car hit the tree.

In passive voice, the action of the verb is happening to the subject of the sentence. For example,

> The student was arrested by the officer.
> The tree was hit by the car.

(*iv*) *Mood*

Verbs also change form to indicate one of the three moods used in English: indicative, imperative, or subjunctive.

A sentence in the indicative mood is a statement. For example,

> She spoke to Robert.
> Lisa drives carefully.

A sentence in the imperative mood is a command or request. For example,

> Stop right there!
> Send the paperwork now.

A sentence in the subjunctive mood expresses an uncertainty, a wish, or a condition contrary to the fact. In subjunctive mood, the verb forms "am", "is", and "are" change to "be". The verb "was" changes to "were", and "has" changes to "have". Verbs ending in "s" drop the "s" when the verb is used in the subjunctive mood. For example,

Uncertainty:
> If he were more convincing, the suspect could be identified.

Wish:
> The winner take all.

Condition contrary to the fact:
> If it were possible, he would escape.

The subjunctive mood is also used in a clause beginning with the word "that" and containing a verb of command, a recommendation, or a parliamentary motion in the main clause. For example,

Command:
> I demand that the accused be released immediately.

Recommendation:
I suggest that the evidence remain in storage.
Parliamentary motion:
I move that the motion be carried.

(c) Verbals

Verbals are words derived from verbs, but are not used as verbs in sentences. There are three kinds of verbals: infinitives, participles, and gerunds.

An infinitive is formed by using "to be" and the verb. Infinitives may be used as nouns, adjectives, or adverbs. For example,

To survive is important. (infinitive as noun)
This is the only way to travel. (infinitive as adjective)
His computer is difficult to operate. (infinitive as adverb)

A participle is used as an adjective to describe a noun. There are two types of participles: present and past. For example,

The running man was stopped by the witness. (present participle)
He was a wanted man. (past participle)

A gerund is formed by adding "ing" to the verb. Gerunds function as nouns in a sentence. For example,

Running is hard work.
The waiting was monotonous.

3. RECOGNIZING AND CORRECTING SENTENCE FRAGMENTS

A sentence contains a subject and a verb and expresses a complete thought. A fragment is an incomplete sentence. Although fragments may be used in novels or in magazine articles, they are not acceptable in formal or business writing. Examples of fragments are:

While chasing the stolen car.
Charges of assault increasing yearly.

Sounded the alarm.
Because it was raining and the driving was treacherous.

To recognize a sentence fragment, check to see if the sentence has a subject and a verb. Remember that the subject will be a noun or a pronoun. The verb will be an action word that explains what the subject is doing. If the verb is not an action word, it will be a form of "to be" followed by a completing word or phrase, or followed by an action verb ending in "ing".

Next, check to see if the sentence expresses a complete thought. Sometimes a sentence can have a subject and a verb without expressing a complete thought. This is called a "dependent clause", which is a type of sentence fragment if it stands alone.

Fortunately, dependent (or subordinate) clauses are easy to recognize. They begin with connecting words such as

after, although, and, as, because, before, by, even, how, if, in, once, unless, until, what, when, whenever, where, which, while

These words are called "subordinate conjunctions". When a clause begins with a subordinate conjunction, the clause is a dependent clause and the thought expressed is incomplete and creates a sentence fragment.

Incomplete thought (Dependent):
Until you get a search warrant.
Complete thought (Independent):
Until you get a search warrant, you can't open the vault.

There are two ways to correct sentence fragments. The first way is to rewrite the fragment to make it a complete sentence. For example,

Fragment — Loitering in the shopping mall.

This fragment lacks a subject and has an "ing" verb (the present participle) without an auxiliary verb.

Rewrite — The suspect was loitering in the shopping mall.

The sentence now has the subject "suspect" and the present participle "loitering" completed with the auxiliary verb "was".

The second way to correct a fragment is to join the fragment to a complete sentence. For example,

Fragment — Although the police were called.

This fragment is a dependent clause, which must be linked to a sentence to make it complete.

Rewrite — Although the police were called, the demonstration continued.

The fragment has been joined to a complete sentence, which is also called an "independent clause". Notice that a comma is placed after the introductory dependent clause. The dependent clause may also be placed after the independent clause. If this order is used, no comma is required.

Another Rewrite — The demonstration continued although the police were called.

4. RECOGNIZING AND CORRECTING RUN-ON SENTENCES

If there is not enough information included in a sentence, a fragment is formed. If too much information is included in a sentence, a run-on sentence (also known as a "fused" sentence) could be formed. A run-on sentence consists of two or more complete sentences written as one sentence, with no punctuation separating each complete sentence. Length is not an indication of a run-on sentence.

Run-on:

Drive safely it is snowing.

Corrected:

Drive safely. It is snowing.

Run-on:

Your duties are not confined to simply enforcing the laws you must also act as a writer, a public speaker, and a witness.

Corrected:

Your duties are not confined to simply enforcing the laws. You must also act as a writer, a public speaker, and a witness.

Incorrect punctuation of a sentence may also result in a run-on sentence. If two complete sentences are joined with a comma, this creates an error known as a "comma splice". A comma splice is another type of run-on sentence.

Comma splice:

The complainant reported excessive noise at a neighbour's party, it was quiet when Constable Simmons arrived.

Corrected:

The complainant reported excessive noise at a neighbour's party. It was quiet when Constable Simmons arrived.

There are five ways to correct run-on sentences. These methods are as follows:

1. Divide the run-on sentence into separate complete sentences by adding periods at the end of each complete sentence.

Run-on:

The child had a broken arm he was transported to the hospital.

Corrected:

The child had a broken arm. He was transported to the hospital.

2. Divide the run-on sentence into separate complete sentences by adding a semicolon to the end of the first complete sentence if it is closely related to the next sentence.

Run-on:

The brown Ford was reported stolen it was found a week later.

Corrected:

The brown Ford was reported stolen; it was found a week later.

3. Two sentences cannot be joined with a comma. However, a comma may be used if it is accompanied by a "co-ordinate conjunction".

The co-ordinate conjunctions are *for, and, nor, but, or, yet, so.* Remember the co-ordinate conjunctions by using the acronym FANBOYS:

F — for
A — and
N — nor
B — but
O — or
Y — yet
S — so

When a co-ordinate conjunction is used to join sentences correctly and to avoid run-ons, a comma precedes the co-ordinate conjunction.

Run-on:
The driver exceeded the speed limit he caused the accident.
Corrected:
The driver exceeded the speed limit, and he caused the accident.

4. **Use a word such as "however", "moreover", "nevertheless", "still", "then", "whereas", or "therefore" to join the sentences in a run-on. These words are called "conjunctive adverbs". If a conjunctive adverb is used to join the sentences, a semicolon must precede the word and a comma must follow it.**

Run-on:
It was difficult to find qualified applicants the deadline was extended.
Corrected:
It was difficult to find qualified applicants; therefore, the deadline was extended.

5. **Change one of the sentences to a dependent clause by adding a subordinate conjunction to the beginning of the sentence.**

Run-on:
The prisoner escaped from custody he was captured quickly.
Corrected:
Although the prisoner escaped from custody, he was captured quickly.

If sentences are not formed correctly, the ideas being expressed will be difficult for the reader to understand. If the reader cannot understand the ideas, the writing will be ineffective.

5. AVOIDING SENTENCE PROBLEMS

(a) Agreement

In order for a sentence to be grammatically correct, the subject and the verb must agree in both person and number. If the subject and verb do not agree, the sentence can be confusing and awkward. For example,

Incorrect Number:
The cases was dismissed.

Incorrect Person:
The police officer am ready for action.

If the subject in the sentence is singular, the verb must also be singular. If the subject is plural, then the verb must also be plural. Therefore, the sentences from the previous example would be corrected to

The cases were dismissed. OR The case was dismissed.
The police officer is ready for action. OR Police officers are ready for action.

In order to recognize agreement problems in sentences, follow these guidelines:

1. Do not allow additional words or phrases to hide the subject of the sentence.

One of the boys (is, are) guilty.

Which verb is correct in this sentence? "Of the boys" is a prepositional phrase that does not contain the subject. Therefore, the subject is "one", which is singular. The singular verb "is" matches the singular subject.

One of the boys is guilty.

2. Compound subjects take plural verbs.

Again, choose the correct verb:

The boy and the girl (was, were) injured.

"Boy and girl" make a plural subject. If in doubt about whether the subject is singular or plural, substitute a pronoun. "Boy and girl" could be replaced with the pronoun "they", which is plural. Therefore, the plural verb "were" matches the plural subject.

The boy and the girl were injured.

3. Watch out for subjects joined by "or".

The revolver or the bullet (is, are) missing.

The "or" signifies that you are referring to only one of the subjects. Either the revolver is missing OR the bullet is missing. Just ONE of them is missing. Therefore, you need the singular verb "is".

The revolver or the bullet is missing.

However, if one of the subjects joined by "either . . . or" or "neither . . . nor" is plural, then the verb agrees with the closest subject.

The lawyer or the witnesses were in the hall.
The witnesses or the lawyer was in the hall.
Either the door or the windows were used to gain entry.
Either the windows or the door was used to gain entry.

4. "Here" and "there" are never subjects.

In this case, the subject of the sentence will be found after the verb, but the verb must still agree with the subject.

There is the woman who escaped.
Here are the stolen cars.

5. Units of money and measurement generally take singular verbs.

Two hundred dollars was removed from the safe.
Sixty miles is difficult to patrol efficiently.

However, if the money or measurements are being considered as separate units, then the verb is plural.

The six suspicious cigarettes are being held as evidence.
The kilometres are recorded on the odometer.

6. **A collective noun (a word that describes a group of people or things) takes a singular verb if the group is considered as one unit.**

Collective nouns include:

army	audience	class
committee	couple	crowd
department	faculty	group
jury	majority	public

The audience is noisy.
The jury is being selected.

However, when the collective nouns are used to refer to all of the individuals within the group, the plural verb is used.

The class are working individually at the computer terminals.
The committee are drinking their coffee.

7. **Some nouns are always singular even though they might appear to be plural.**

Words such as

physics, news, mathematics, statistics, economics, athletics, ethics, politics, whereabouts

always take singular verbs.

His whereabouts is unknown.
Economics is an important subject.

Other nouns, usually thought of as "a pair of", take plural verbs. These words include

scissors, trousers, pliers, handcuffs, gloves, tweezers, glasses.

The tweezers are in the top drawer.
The scissors were on my desk.

8. While "personal pronouns" replace nouns in a sentence (*e.g.*, the personal pronoun "he" could replace "the man"), there are other pronouns that are more general.

These "indefinite pronouns" include:

all	any	anybody
anyone	anything	both
each	either	enough
everybody	everyone	few
less	little	many
more	most	much
neither	nobody	none
no one	one	plenty
several	some	somebody
someone	something	

Most indefinite pronouns except "both", "few", "many", and "several" take singular verbs. The indefinite pronouns "all", "any", "enough", "more", "most", "none", "plenty", and "some" can take either a singular or a plural verb, depending on what the pronoun is replacing in the sentence. The pronouns "less", "little", and "much" are used only to refer to quantity or portion.

Singular

Anyone is a suspect.
No one is willing to give a statement.
Something is missing.
All is quiet.
Most of the room has been checked.
Little is known about the masked gunman.

Plural

Both of the officers are at the scene.
Few of the clues were needed to verify his identity.
Several witnesses were questioned.
Many leads are being investigated.
All of the guns are loaded.
Most of the rules have been broken.

When you are using an indefinite pronoun such as *each, everyone,* and *everybody,* remind yourself that you are referring to "each and every single one", or "each and every single body".

> Each of the victims is in court. (Each and every single one of the victims is in court.)
> Everybody is upset. (Each and every single body is upset.)

9. Personal pronouns follow the same rules as nouns. If you can substitute "I", "you", "he", "she", or "it" for the noun, use the singular form of the verb. If you can substitute "we" or "they" for the noun, use the plural form of the verb.

> The judge looks tired. — He looks tired.
> The judges are in agreement. — They are in agreement.

Pronouns must also agree with the subject if they are used to replace the subject later in the sentence.

> Harold complained about his assignment.
> Everyone brought his own beer.

Note: In an attempt to make writing gender-free, writers sometimes use "he/she" or "his/her" if the gender of the subject of the sentence is not known. For example

> The student brought his/her book to class.

While this eliminates the gender bias, it makes the sentence awkward. A better method of eliminating gender would be to change the singular subject to a plural, such as

> The students brought their books to class.

(b) Shifts of Person

Although pronouns can replace nouns, you cannot jump from one pronoun to another and expect the reader to know that you are still referring to the same noun. One of the most common errors in writing is the unnecessary shifting from one group of pronouns to another.

There are three groups of pronouns or "persons" in English.

PERSON	SINGULAR	PLURAL
First	I	we
Second	you	you
Third	he/she/it/one	they

(*i*) *First person*

It is common to write in the first person if you are describing a personal event. In this case, you would use the first person singular.

I was driving to the gas station when the car stalled.

If the event included someone else, or a group of people, you could still use first person; however, you now need the first person plural.

We will wait for the rest of the team before we begin to practise.

(*ii*) *Second person*

Second person is used to talk directly to the reader. "You" is used to give directions or to make the tone of writing informal and friendly. "You" can be both singular and plural. The pronoun "you" could refer to one person or to a group of people.

You shouldn't handle firearms carelessly.
You are invited to graduation ceremonies at the police college.

(*iii*) *Third person*

This group of pronouns is used to describe someone else's actions. The pronoun can be singular:

He is planning to appeal the case.
She is being detained.
It has been identified as the murder weapon.
One must learn the rules.

It can also be plural:

They turned into an ugly mob when the concert was cancelled.

(iv) Avoid shifts of person

Problems are created when you change from one group of pronouns to another. These changes can be confusing. For example,

If you want to get a promotion, one should study.

Here, the writer has shifted from "you" to "one". "You" is second person but "one" is third person. Do these pronouns refer to the same individual? The reader cannot be sure. The sentence should be revised by choosing either second or third person.

If you want to get a promotion, you should study. (second person)
If one wants to get a promotion, one should study. (third person)

The sentence could also be changed to first person.

If I want to get a promotion, I should study.

If you are required to write in the third person, be careful that you do not lapse into first person (*I* or *we*) or second person (*you*). For example,

At 22:00 hours when he arrived, I made the following observations: the accused was unsteady on his feet, his speech was slurred, his eyes were glazed and he smelled strongly of an alcoholic beverage. At 22:10 hours, you formed the opinion that the accused's ability to operate the motor vehicle was impaired by alcohol. He was arrested, cautioned, and read his rights to counsel. After I placed him in the police vehicle, he was read the formal breath demand.

The report would be clearer if it avoided shifts of person.

At 22:00 hours P.C. Coles arrived and made the following observations: the accused was unsteady on his feet, his speech was slurred, his eyes were glazed and he smelled strongly of an alcoholic beverage. At 22:10 hours, the officer formed the opinion that the accused's ability to operate the motor vehicle was impaired by alcohol. The accused was arrested, cautioned, and read his rights to counsel. After being placed in the police vehicle, he was read the formal breath demand.

(c) Pronoun Problems

Many writers include unnecessary pronouns. For writing that must be formal, pronouns are often eliminated entirely. For example,

> You will notice that a staff sergeant must read many reports.

The phrase "you will notice" could be omitted.

> A staff sergeant must read many reports.

As well, overusing the third person pronoun "one" can make writing stuffy and pretentious.

> One should always be cautious when one approaches an abandoned vehicle.

This sentence could be changed to the second person.

> You should be cautious when approaching an abandoned vehicle.

This sentence could also be changed by eliminating the pronouns altogether.

> Caution should be used when approaching an abandoned vehicle.
>
> or
>
> Use caution when approaching an abandoned vehicle.
>
> or
>
> Approach an abandoned vehicle cautiously.

Choose the method that is the most appropriate for the purpose of your writing or the method required by your department.

(d) Misplaced Modifiers

Modifiers are words used to make a sentence more descriptive or specific. Modifiers can be various parts of speech. The meaning of the sentence will change depending on where the modifier is positioned in the sentence. Look at this sentence:

> I spoke to the police officer.

When the modifier "ONLY" is added at different positions in the sentence, the meaning of the sentence also changes.

> ONLY I spoke to the police officer.
> I ONLY spoke to the police officer.
> I spoke to ONLY the police officer.
> I spoke to the ONLY police officer.
> I spoke to the police officer ONLY.

Unfortunately, if the modifying word or phrase is not positioned correctly, the sentence can both embarrass the writer and confuse the reader. Read the following sentences and try to recognize the problems caused by misplaced modifiers.

1. What made the beach interesting was the scenery walking around.
2. He laughed in my face and threw it in the wastepaper basket.
3. The man was murdered with his wallet in the car.
4. The victim wore a ribbon in her hair which was velvet.

Try to correct the sentences so that they are not confusing or misleading. See if your corrections match these:

1. The scenery we noticed when we walked around made the beach interesting.
2. He laughed in my face and threw the summons in the wastepaper basket.
3. The man was murdered in the car. His wallet was found in the glove compartment.
4. The victim wore a velvet ribbon in her hair.

When writing, it is important to be precise and not mislead the reader, otherwise your ideas could be misinterpreted. Here are some guidelines for avoiding misplaced modifiers:

1. Place the modifying word or phrase beside the word or phrase it modifies.

Incorrect:

Lost and crying, the policeman called for help for the little girl.

Correct:

The policeman called for help for the *lost and crying* little girl.

2. Be careful with pronouns.

Pronouns are used to replace nouns, and they always refer to the noun that immediately precedes them. The pronouns *he, she, it,* and *they* or the possessive pronouns *his, hers, its,* and *theirs* cause problems when they refer to the incorrect noun. This is called "faulty pronoun reference".

Incorrect:

> The judge decided he was insane when he murdered the movie star. (Was the judge the insane murderer? The pronoun "he" now refers to the noun "judge".)

Correct:

> The judge decided that the defendant was insane when he murdered the movie star.

3. Use the pronouns "I" and "me" correctly.

The pronouns "I" and "me" can also cause problems. "I" is used as the subject of the sentence.

> I was assigned to foot patrol.

"Me" is always used as an object, and is usually located at the end of the sentence.

> The foot patrol assignment was given to me.

To check whether to use "I" or "me" in combination with other subjects or objects, eliminate the extra words in the following sentence:

> The homicide should be reported to Constable Wright or to
>
> __________.

Take out the phrase "Constable Wright or" from the sentence. It would be incorrect to write "reported to I", so the correct word for the sentence would be "me".

> The homicide should be reported to Constable Wright or to me.

(e) Other Modifier Problems

Modifiers can cause other sentence problems. When modifiers are not used correctly, ideas are not communicated clearly. To prevent modifier problems, follow these guidelines:

1. Use "good" and "well" correctly.

"Good" is an adjective. It describes a noun.

A good vacation includes sun and sand.

"Well" is an adverb. It describes a verb.

The child complained that he did not feel well.

2. Learn to use the correct comparison.

There are three forms of comparison: "positive", "comparative", and "superlative". The "positive" is the form of a word when it is used alone. The "comparative" form compares two things. The "superlative" form compares three or more things. Most adjectives and adverbs are formed by adding "er" or "est" to the positive form. Sometimes "more" or "most" (or "less" or "least") are used.

Positive Form:
The car moved RAPIDLY.

Comparative Form:
The green car moved MORE RAPIDLY than the red car.

Superlative Form:
In the race, the winning car moved MOST RAPIDLY.

Look at another example:

Sergeant Smith is tall. (positive)
Sergeant Smith is taller than his partner. (comparative)
Sergeant Smith is the tallest member of the team. (superlative)

Irregular Comparatives:
a) bad — This is a bad headache. (positive)
worse — This headache is worse than the one I had yesterday. (comparative)

worst — This is the worst headache I've ever had. (superlative)

b) good — He did a good job. (positive)
better — He did a better job than his partner. (comparative)
best — He did the best job in the unit. (superlative)

c) many — She has many friends. (positive)
more — She has more friends than Louise. (comparative)
most — She has the most friends of any girl in the room. (superlative)

Watch for words that cannot be compared, such as

unique, perfect, dead, empty, exact, viable.

3. Eliminate unnecessary modifiers.

Avoid repeating an idea by using unnecessary modifiers. This does not strengthen the idea; it only makes the sentence longer, increases the chance for error, and annoys many readers. Watch for phrases such as:

"Viable solution" — If it is a solution then it must be viable. "Viable alternative" is just as bad. Omit the word "viable".

"Fact of the matter" — This phrase could be shortened to one word such as the "situation", or the "cause", or the "fact".

(f) Parallel Structure

When items are described in a series, the same parts of speech must be used to achieve parallel structure. Balance nouns with nouns, phrases with phrases, and clauses with clauses. Parallel structure is an effective device for emphasizing information and for making sentences orderly.

Often, similar items are described in the same sentence. Correct parallel structure must be used to make the description more effective. For example,

Incorrect:

Computers help us to gather statistics and improving writing skills.

Parallel:

Computers help us to gather statistics and to improve our writing skills.

Incorrect:

Earl enjoys gambling, drink, and to drive fast cars.

Parallel:

Earl enjoys gambling, drinking, and driving fast cars.

Parallel structure is important when items are listed. For example,

Incorrect:

This report will examine
a) using policies and procedures;
b) how in-service training works; and
c) are there restrictions on the budget.

Parallel:

This report will examine
a) policies and procedures;
b) in-service training practices; and
c) budget restrictions.

Follow these guidelines to avoid problems with parallel structure:

1. Reinforce the structure by repeating the introductory word.

Weak:

Herman produced a poster, brochure, and a newsletter.

Stronger:

Herman produced a poster, a brochure, and a newsletter.

2. Use "correlatives" to connect parallel elements in a sentence.

CORRELATIVE	EXAMPLE
Both . . . and	Both power and authority are tempting.
Either . . . or	The poor conditions will be either magnified or solved by management.

Neither . . . nor	Neither spelling problems nor grammatical errors spoiled the analysis.
Not only . . . but also	We judge applicants not only by their academic record but also by their physical fitness.
Whether . . . or	Whether the crime was committed in this sector or elsewhere, it remains your responsibility.

3. **Gender should also be treated without bias when forming parallel structure.**

Weak:

The men from the squad and the girls from the office organized the retirement dinner.

Parallel:

The men from the squad and the women from the office organized the retirement dinner.

Another correction is to remove the gender reference entirely. For example,

The squad members and the office workers organized the retirement dinner.

8

Style

While correct grammar is important to good writing, clear communication depends on the way ideas are expressed. English is a very flexible language, and there are many different ways to express similar ideas. Style describes the way words are put together and the effect created.

1. CHOOSE AN APPROPRIATE STYLE

Style in writing can be compared to style in relation to clothing. Style changes depending on the circumstances. For some occasions, it would be appropriate to opt for a casual style of dress such as jeans and a T-shirt. For other occasions, more formal attire is required. In addition, each person wears clothing with a unique personal style. For some occasions, writing may have a personal flair. In other circumstances, writing must conform exactly to a standard format.

Just as the required style of dress for police officers on duty is a uniform, there is a style of writing that is appropriate for police documents. The police report is not the place to insist on exercising a creative and personal style of writing. On the other hand, just as there are occasions when it would be inappropriate to wear a police uniform, there are occasions when it would be inappropriate to write using a "police style".

Style in writing involves the level of formality of word choice and the tone created by the language. To choose a writing style that is appropriate, consider the purpose of the writing. The basic purpose of all writing is to communicate ideas or information from the writer to the reader. More specifically, writing can also inform, describe, define, compare, persuade, or explain. Knowing the purpose of the writing will help you to determine what content should be included, how the content should be organized, and what wording will be most effective.

For example, writing designed to inform must be complete, clear, and precise. Writing designed to persuade calls for careful attention to organization in order to lead the reader to a specific decision or action. To determine the purpose of writing, ask yourself why you are writing. What do you want to accomplish?

Another consideration in determining the correct style is the audience. Who will read what you have written? Some forms of writing, such as business letters, are written for one specific reader. Other types of writing, such as journal articles or police reports, are written for a wider audience. Knowing the audience helps to determine the level of formality and the tone required in a piece of writing. Generally, a formal writing style is appropriate for a wide audience. If your writing is to be read by a single reader, consider your relationship with that reader. If you know the reader well, you may choose to use an informal, "chatty" style. This is most commonly seen in email. However, if your relationship with the reader is professional rather than personal, a formal style is preferable even in an email.

The required tone determines the level of formality. To establish a business-like and professional tone, a formal writing style must be used. To create a friendly and personal tone, an informal writing style would be required. If an overly formal style is used, the reader may feel that the writing is cold, stuffy, and pompous. If an inappropriately informal style is used, the reader may feel that the writing is too casual and that the writer is not taking the topic seriously. In both of these examples, the tone created by the writing style is not correct for the situation and reflects poorly on the writer.

A formal writing style is achieved by using correct wording rather than slang. For example, it is more formal to use "children" rather than "kids". Contractions should also be avoided. Formal writing must be correct in all aspects of writing mechanics, including punctuation, grammar, spelling, usage, and sentence structure. While broken sentences and "innovative" punctuation may be acceptable in informal writing, they are not acceptable in business or professional writing.

A formal writing style is not achieved by loading the writing with jargon or unnecessary words. For example, it is not more formal to write "at this point in time" instead of "now", or to use "premises" instead of "house". In fact, using extra words or jargon only obscures the meaning. Clarity in the communication of ideas is essential for a formal writing style and demonstrates the professionalism of the writer.

2. CONCISE, COMPLETE, AND COHERENT WRITING

An appropriate style in writing is sensitive to the reader. In any business, including the business of police work, readers are busy people and appreciate concise writing that transmits only the information necessary to accomplish the purpose of the writing. Therefore, the reader's time is not wasted.

Concise writing does not have to sound like a telegram: "Arrived 10:50. Searched area. Found nothing." However, it must express information precisely. Include only relevant information, and do not repeat an idea after it has been presented. Organize information logically so that the reader can follow the ideas presented or visualize the actions described.

To make sentences concise, avoid beginning them with phrases such as "There is" or "There are." In the following example, notice how changing the beginning of the sentence makes it more concise:

Original:
There are six vicious dogs in the building.
Revised:
Six vicious dogs are in the building.

The revised version has the subject of the sentence at the beginning. Look at this example in terms of word length:

Original:
There is a flat tire on the car to which I was assigned.
Revised:
I was assigned to a car with a flat tire.

The first sentence has 13 words; the second sentence has only 10.

To make sentences concise, remove repetitive words. For example:

1. don't use "more" or "most" with words that already have defined limits (*incorrect* — more straight, most equal, more unique, most perfect);
2. don't use "more" or "most" with words ending in "er" or "est" (*incorrect* — more faster, most oldest, more duller, most strongest);
3. don't use "again" with verbs beginning with "re" (*incorrect* — resubmit again, restart again, repeat again, rerun again).

Unfortunately, writers fail to trust the strength of words and attempt to reinforce ideas by repeating them. Frequently, redundant expressions creep into popular use. For example, the phrase "viable solution" appears to be acceptable; however, when the phrase is examined, it is clear that "viable" is redundant to the word "solution". If something is viable, then it must be a solution. If it is not viable, then it cannot be a solution. Other common redundant expressions include:

> separate out, rise up, co-operate together, many in number, return back, visible to the eye, necessary and essential, 6 a.m. in the morning, complete control, exact replica

Another cause of excess wording is the use of double expressions. For example, "this report or study" could be shortened to "this report" or to "this study". "Cease and desist" could be shortened to "cease" or "desist" or, even better, "stop". "For all intents and purposes" could be changed to "for all purposes" or, in most cases, it could be eliminated altogether. However, concise writing must also be complete. All of the essential information must be included so that the reader is not left with unanswered questions. For example, a report which states

> Investigated burglary. No arrest.

is concise, but not complete. More information is needed. Where are the answers to "Who, What, Where, When, Why, How"? How could any follow-up be based on this information?

Most police writing is done on pre-printed forms that indicate what information should be included. Unfortunately, the form report system is effective only if the information provided by the investigating officer is complete. For example, General Occurrence Report forms provide a box marked "Location of Occurrence". If the location of an occurrence is given as "Joe's Fruit Market", the information might not be complete. Will everyone who reads the report know the location of Joe's Fruit Market? Obviously, the addition of an address is essential to make the "Location of Occurrence" complete.

To determine whether writing is complete, answer all of the questions the reader might ask. Make sure that all information necessary to satisfy every legal requirement is included. In an arrest report, it is essential to note that the accused was advised of his or her rights. In a memo announcing a meeting, provide the date, time, and location. The reader is not a psychic who can fill in what has been left out.

An effective style makes writing easy to read. Coherent writing is easier to read than writing that is disorganized and choppy. In well-organized writing, each thought leads logically to the next. It is the writer's job to organize the information so that the reader can understand it. Organized writing is coherent because each idea follows logically from the preceding one and leads smoothly to the next one. Use the following guidelines to help you to improve your organization:

1. Arrange information in a logical order.

Choose an order that is appropriate for the information. For example,

ORDER	INTENDED PURPOSE
front to back	to describe a house
top to bottom	to describe a person
outside to inside	to describe a car
most valuable to least valuable	to make a list of burglarized items
beginning to end	to describe an occurrence

2. Keep verb tenses consistent.

Jumping from past to present to future and back to the past spoils coherence. The reader will not be able to follow the time sequence. The verbs are the key to expressing the chronological order of events.

Incorrect:

I am walking near the park when I will notice a body behind the trees.

Correct:

I was walking near the park when I noticed a body behind the trees.

3. Finish one thought before beginning the next.

Speakers often jump from one idea to the next. Gestures and tone of voice help listeners to understand what is said. In writing, this method of indiscriminately adding ideas is unacceptable. In order to ensure that the essential information is included and arranged in the most effective order, make an outline before writing. It is easier to see similar ideas when they are listed in an outline than when they are buried in sentences and paragraphs. Once similar ideas are identified, they can be grouped together to achieve coherence and to avoid repetition.

4. Use transitional words and phrases to link sentences and paragraphs.

Transitional words and phrases make the writing flow smoothly. Link sentences with transitions to give the reader "road signs" to follow the development of ideas.

COMMON TRANSITIONAL WORDS AND PHRASES

although	as
as well	before
besides	but
for example	furthermore
however	in addition to
in conclusion	inevitably
in the meantime	meanwhile
naturally	previously
still	then
until	yet

Transitional words make it easier for the reader to follow the development of ideas. Examine the following passage, which contains no transitions:

Poisonous substances are found in every home. Bleach, antifreeze, paint remover, and cleaning substances are common household products. Children may be injured or even killed if

> they swallow poisons. It is important that you know first aid. You can provide immediate assistance if a child ingests a poison.

It is easier to follow the ideas when transitional words and phrases are added:

> Poisonous substances are found in every home. FOR EXAMPLE, bleach, antifreeze, paint remover and cleaning substances are common household products. UNFORTUNATELY, children may be injured or even killed if they swallow THESE poisons. THEREFORE, it is important that you know first aid SO THAT you can provide immediate assistance if a child ingests a poison.

Paragraphs can also be linked by using transitional words in the opening sentences of new paragraphs. This is effective, but it can become repetitive if each new paragraph begins with a transitional word or phrase. To avoid this monotony, especially in long reports or research papers, many writers repeat a key word or idea from the last sentence of a paragraph in the first sentence of the next paragraph. If the last sentence of the paragraph is "Good supervisors are required to provide adequate motivation" the next paragraph could begin with the sentence "Motivation is a concern of good managers." In this case, repetition of the word "motivation" links the paragraphs and provides coherence.

3. STYLE: A CHECKLIST

Style can be improved by revising words, sentences, and paragraphs. Use the following checklist to help you to strengthen your writing style.

(a) Choose the Best Words

1. Eliminate unnecessary words.

Do not force sentences to carry unnecessary baggage. Change long expressions such as "at this point in time" to shorter ones such as "now".

2. Use active rather than passive verbs.

Verbs carry the action in the sentences; therefore, it is important to keep verbs lively and precise. By using the active voice, you make the subject of the sentence perform the action directly rather than indirectly. Write "Fred hit Marvin" (active voice) rather than "Marvin was hit by Fred" (passive voice).

3. Choose specific and accurate words.

Specific and accurate word choice gives the reader a clearer understanding of the information. For example, it is easier to visualize a "1995 Ford Escort" than "a vehicle". Vague terms such as "seriously injured" leave the reader wondering about the extent of the injuries. It would be clearer to describe the injuries as "extensive cuts to the face, three broken ribs, and a crushed arm."

4. Eliminate qualifiers.

Do not flirt with ideas. Write "This causes . . ." rather than "In some cases, this may frequently cause . . . ". Delete redundant words from expressions. Change a "short summary" to "summary" and "very unique" to "unique".

5. Keep wording natural.

Simple writing is effective. Impress readers with your ideas and information instead of confusing them with your extensive vocabulary. Change "Kindly direct me to my habitual abode" to "Please show me the way home."

(b) Write Strong Sentences

1. Vary your sentence length.

Sentences of the same length are monotonous. Short sentences can emphasize information, and long sentences can be used to explain ideas fully.

2. Put important ideas first or last.

Important information should not be buried in the middle of sentences. Avoid long introductory phrases. For example, change "After the training course sponsored by the Education Department, reports improved so the course was a success" to "Reports improved after the Education Department sponsored the successful training course." Action is also encouraged when emphasis is placed at the end of the sentence (for example, "Do it NOW").

3. Keep sentence structure simple.

The basic structure of sentences in English is "Subject/Verb/ Object". For example, "The child destroyed the bicycle." To achieve variety in sentence structure, an introductory phrase is often used. For example, "After the party, the child destroyed the bicycle." However, other sentence structure patterns may make the sentences complicated and difficult to understand. Too many phrases within a sentence are confusing and cause punctuation problems. For example, "These statistics, which have been taken from the annual report, may, to some readers, indicate that the changes have not been successful" could be changed to "To some readers, these statistics from the annual report may indicate that the changes have not been successful." Simple sentences are easier to write and easier to read.

4. Use parallel structure correctly.

Parallel structure gives a sentence balance. Make sure that each parallel element in a sentence has the same structure. For example, the sentence "The department lacks vision, integrity, and doesn't have any backbone" lacks parallel structure. Strengthen the parallel structure by revising the sentence to "The department lacks vision, integrity, and courage."

5. Focus on a single idea in each sentence.

When there are too many ideas in one sentence, the sentence loses focus. Each sentence should be a single unit of thought. For example, the sentence "Schools must be responsible for improving the literacy of their students so crime does not increase" is confusing because the relationship between literacy and crime is not clear. Instead, use two separate sentences to develop the ideas clearly: "Studies have shown that there is a relationship between low literacy and crime levels. Therefore, schools can contribute to reducing crime by improving the literacy of their students."

(c) Develop Coherent Paragraphs

1. Use transitional words and phrases.

Transitional words and phrases link the sentences within the paragraph and may also be used to link one paragraph to the next. Therefore, transitions make the paragraph coherent and easy to read.

2. Develop one idea fully in each paragraph.

Each paragraph should contain a topic sentence to explain what the paragraph will be about. The sentences that follow should elaborate on that topic by providing explanations and examples. Finally, the paragraph should have a concluding sentence to make the reader aware of the importance of that specific discussion to the overall topic under discussion.

3. Avoid one-sentence paragraphs.

It is difficult to develop ideas fully in one sentence. A series of one-sentence paragraphs makes writing choppy and incoherent. Again, this problem is often seen in emails. A one-sentence paragraph may serve effectively as a contrast to much longer paragraphs; however, paragraphs should be fully developed.

4. Arrange paragraphs iogically.

Each paragraph provides one unit of information. Individual units, when combined, should build logically to develop an argument, to provide a description, or to give an explanation. The paragraphs must be organized logically so that the reader will be able to follow the development of the ideas.

5. Eliminate irrelevant information.

All of the information within each paragraph must relate to the topic of the paragraph itself and to the topic under discussion. The reader will not want to waste time reading paragraphs that contain irrelevant information.

(d) Generally

1. Write for your reader.

Remember that you are not writing for yourself. Clear writing shows professionalism by recognizing and respecting the reader. Develop a style that commands respect by using appropriate organization, vocabulary, sentence structure, and paragraph development.

2. Include all of the necessary information.

View your writing from the reader's point of view and answer all of the reader's questions. If all of the information the reader requires is not provided, the writing has not done its job.

3. Be courteous.

Good manners are important to good style. A memo or letter that neglects simple elements, such as "please" and "thank you", is not commanding; it is rude.

PART THREE
ESSAYS AND RESEARCH PAPERS

9

Essays and Research Papers

1. WHEN WILL YOU WRITE AN ESSAY OR RESEARCH PAPER?

Police departments have traditionally encouraged their officers to pursue post-secondary studies or in-service training courses. Essays and research papers are often a major segment of the grading scheme in such courses. By writing a good paper, you can demonstrate a broad knowledge of the course content or in-depth knowledge of one specific area of the course.

Essays are used by many police services as part of the promotional assessment process. When writing an essay, you will be expected to demonstrate insight into the topic assigned and to express your ideas in a clear, logical manner.

When you write a research paper, you gain the opportunity to compare your ideas with those of experts in the field. You also discover sources of information that may prove useful to you in the future.

Your research paper could also form the basis of an article that could be published in a police magazine. This, certainly, enhances your reputation as an expert in your field.

2. THE ESSAY EXAMINATION: WRITING ESSAYS FOR PROMOTIONS

Many police services use essays as part of the evaluation that forms the basis for decisions about promotions. These essays are similar to the papers that may be required on examinations in academic courses. The writer does not know the topic before writing the essay, the writing is supervised and has a time limit, and the writer has no access to outside sources of information.

Under these circumstances, the essay must be planned and written quickly while still demonstrating that the writer has a good command of language and an understanding of the information discussed. In order to complete an examination essay successfully, good time management is essential.

There are four basic tasks that must be completed in the allotted time. First, an approach to the topic must be devised; then an outline must be written to ensure that all of the information is included and arranged in the most effective and logical order. After the outline has been completed, the essay itself must be written. Finally, the essay must be revised and proofread before it is submitted.

To manage time successfully, each of these four steps should take a designated percentage of the total test time. In general, deciding on the topic (or how to focus on the assigned topic if no choice is allowed) should take approximately 10% of the time. Writing the outline should take 20%. Writing the essay should take 50%. The revision and proofreading should take 20%. Therefore, if the test is to be completed in ninety minutes, divide the time approximately as follows:

10 minutes — determine the approach to the topic (10%)
20 minutes — write the outline (20%)
40 minutes — write the essay (50%)
20 minutes — revise and proofread (20%)

This four-step process makes time management easier and prevents you from wasting time at the beginning of the test and scrambling to finish in the last few minutes. It also helps you to write an essay that is thoughtful, well planned, and clearly expressed. Each step contributes to the success of the final essay.

(a) Step 1: Examine the Topic

There are two types of topics that are frequently used for promotion essays. The first type of topic is the "scenario". For example, the topic could be "There has been a toxic spill in your patrol zone. Explain the procedure that should be followed." The other type of topic is a general discussion. For example: "Explain how the role of the police officer will change with the implementation of community-based policing."

To determine the best approach to the topic, examine the topic carefully and find the sections that could be discussed within the major topic. The traditional approach to examination essays relies on the use of three major sections. While more sections could be included, most topics divide easily into three sections. Too many sections could result in a confused essay that would not be coherent or well developed.

Notice how both types of essay topics, the scenario and the discussion, can be divided into three areas. If you were required to complete the toxic spill essay, the topic could be divided into

a) preparation for evacuation;
b) the evacuation itself; and
c) post-evacuation.

If you were required to discuss the impact of community-based policing, the topic could be divided into

a) the traditional role of the police officer;
b) the goals of community-based policing; and
c) the way the traditional role is going to be changed by the community-based programme.

Once you know how you will approach the topic, the next step is to organize ideas within the three established subsections.

(b) Step 2: Write the Outline

Resist the temptation to skip the outline stage in order to get on with writing the essay. The outline allows you to organize your ideas in an effective order and to develop each observation fully. It also builds in a safety net; if the three sections do not work well, or if you cannot develop any of the sections, the problem will be obvious after a few minutes of working on the outline rather than half-way through the essay itself, when it is too late to change the approach to the topic.

Again, for each of the sections in your topic breakdown, add three supporting ideas or subsections. It is easier to work with the same number of sections and subsections since this keeps the essay evenly balanced and saves the time it would take to determine how many ideas to include. For example,

Toxic Spill Essay

a) Preparation for evacuation
   — training officers before the emergency
   — providing emergency shelter and health care
   — methods of announcing the evacuation

b) The evacuation itself
   — effective use of personnel and resources
   — methods of reducing traffic problems and ensuring the speed of the operation
   — methods of reducing crime during the evacuation

c) Post-evacuation
   — designating responsibility for protecting the toxic site and the evacuated community
   — criteria for declaring the area safe
   — methods of returning people to the area safely.

Role of the Police Essay

a) The traditional role of the police officer
   — the use of "reactive" procedures
   — police isolation from the community
   — resulting police attitude to the community

b) The goals of community-based policing
   — involving the community in crime prevention programmes
   — developing stronger ties between the community and the police
   — strengthening the image of the police

c) Changes to the role of the police

- — lessening specialization
- — building better communication skills
- — increasing job satisfaction

Once you are satisfied with the outline, trust it. Under test conditions, it is not advantageous to change the ideas in the outline or to change the arrangement of the ideas. When the outline is complete, it is a simple process to transfer the ideas from the outline into the sentences and paragraphs required in the essay.

(c) Step 3: Write The Essay

The outline will provide the body of the essay. However, the essay still needs an opening paragraph and a closing paragraph to make it complete. If each of the sections in the body consists of one paragraph, and an opening paragraph and closing paragraph are added, the result will be a five-paragraph essay. A longer essay can be written by developing each of the subsections in the outline as a separate paragraph, but a five-paragraph essay is usually long enough to explain ideas fully under test conditions. If you are unsure about the required length of the essay, ask the instructor.

The opening paragraph defines the scope of the topic to be discussed. Explain the three sections you have covered on the outline and show how each relates to the assigned topic. For example, the "toxic spill" essay could begin

> Every day, toxic materials are shipped through our community by road and rail and, despite safety precautions and regulations, a toxic spill could occur. Careful planning before such an accident, a well-managed evacuation plan, and a clear system for maintaining security after the accident will ensure that such a disaster is handled quickly and safely. When an emergency exists, it is too late to formulate plans and delegate responsibilities.

The "role of the police" essay could begin

> The community-based policing programme will change the role of the police officer. This opportunity challenges the nature of police work and the duties it involves. As the traditional system of policing is modified to meet the goals of the community-based

policing programmes, officers must find new ways to function effectively.

After you have written the opening paragraphs, use the outline to form the body paragraphs of the essay. Expand each idea in the outline to one or two sentences, and give specific support or examples whenever possible. If you follow the outline, the ideas will remain logically organized.

A concluding paragraph provides a summary of the focus of the essay and leaves the reader with a positive impression of the essay, the quality of its ideas, and the clarity of the writing. If you have difficulty developing a concluding paragraph, ask yourself what would happen if the system you have discussed were not put into place. For example: "Unless an efficient emergency plan is developed, a disaster may take an even greater toll both during and after the emergency itself" or "Maintaining the traditional role of the police officer may act as an impediment to the successful implementation of the entire community-based policing programme." Another approach to the conclusion is to point to the future. For example: "The existing emergency plans must be revised in order to meet these objectives and provide adequate protection for the public" or "The community-based policing programme will not only change the role of police officers, it will improve working conditions and enhance professional development."

(d) Step 4: Revise and Proofread

As a result of your careful time management, you will have time after you have finished writing to revise and proofread your work. At this point, it is too late to make radical changes in the essay. However, this step is critical for the removal of careless errors that will undermine the quality of your essay.

The revisions that can be made include strengthening word choice, improving sentence structure, and correcting punctuation. Changes such as these will help to communicate your ideas clearly to the reader.

It is essential to correct spelling errors. Even readers who may miss other types of errors rarely fail to see spelling errors. Take the time to check every word that you may have misspelled. Under test conditions, and while working without the benefit of computer spell check programs or the other sources available to aid spelling, it is easy to allow spelling errors to creep into your work. If you are allowed to use a dictionary, take advantage of this opportunity instead of relying on your own spelling instincts. If you are not allowed to use a dictionary, write the word out and rely on your ability to recognize the familiar spelling.

Proofreading should be a separate task. When you proofread, you are not looking for the things you want to revise. Instead, you are reading the essay to check for missing words, illegible letters and other formatting matters such as page numbering. Follow the assignment instructions carefully. For example, is your name required on every page or just on the cover sheet? You do not want your reader to approach the essay already annoyed that you have not followed simple submission instructions.

3. THE WRITING PROCESS FOR SUCCESSFUL RESEARCH PAPERS

Writing a research paper may appear to be an overwhelming task. Inexperienced writers often procrastinate. As a result, the paper is written in one long, painful marathon session. Unfortunately, this method makes the task of writing the paper difficult. As well, the quality of the writing is poor because not enough time is available to make final corrections or changes. Very few writers, including professional writers, can think, write, and edit simultaneously. Your research papers will be better if you divide the process of writing into small, well-organized sections; then, you can work out a schedule for the completion of each section so that you can manage your time effectively.

TEN STEPS TO A GOOD RESEARCH PAPER

1. Choose a topic.
2. Narrow the topic.
3. Research.
4. Organize your information.
5. Determine your audience.
6. Write the outline.
7. Write a draft.
8. Revise and edit. (Repeat steps 7 and 8 as often as necessary.)

9. Prepare the final copy.
10. Proofread.

(a) Step 1: Choose a Topic

Regardless of how unappealing the topic may appear, you can write a good paper if you organize and research extensively. Although writing about a topic that you find interesting is more enjoyable, it is not a prerequisite to success.

If your instructor has given you a choice of topics, then you must make a decision. Look at the topics again. Do you have any personal experiences that would be relevant to the topic or do you have a contact in that field? Is there a topic that would be helpful or relevant to your career? For example, if you are hoping to be promoted and one of the topics is on management theories, look no further.

Before you make a final decision about your topic, take a quick look through the library or browse the internet. This will prevent you from choosing a topic on which there is little or no supporting information. Discussing your topic with a friend or another student is another good way of testing your ideas and developing your approach to the topic.

(b) Step 2: Narrow the Topic

It is difficult to write a good research paper on a topic that is vague and general. For example, trying to explain all of the aspects of crime prevention in a scant 500 words is frustrating both for the writer and for the reader. To limit and define your topic, use a thesis statement.

A thesis statement is a precisely worded sentence that states the focus of your paper. Like the hypothesis in a scientific experiment, the thesis explains what you are going to show or prove. In science, an experiment is used to develop or prove a hypothesis; in a research paper, a well-organized argument supports your thesis.

Limiting your topic does not mean that there will not be sufficient information available. Often, you will be amazed at how much information is available once you start researching. However, if you find that supporting material is not available in the limited area you have selected, you can still change your thesis before you invest a great deal of time in the paper.

A good thesis will make your research easier. Too many writers wander through the library looking for "something on crime" or "some books for my psychology paper." Knowing exactly what you want will help you to locate information easily and quickly. In this way, you will not spend your time sifting through irrelevant information.

Sometimes it is difficult to decide just how to word your thesis. When you were assigned the topic of the paper, it is likely that you were also assigned a word length. Use this word length as an indication of the required scope of your paper. The shorter the paper, the narrower you should focus your thesis. In general, papers under 1,000 words are considered "short" papers.

For example, you could be given the topic "Motivation". This topic must be narrowed before you can write a good paper about it. First, think of all the areas that you believe contribute to "Motivation"; then, make a list of some of the most interesting areas. Your list might include:

money
promotions
responsibility
independence
social status

Choose one of the major subheadings in the list to begin the process of determining the thesis for your paper.

Assume that you have chosen to examine the area of "Money as a Motivator." This will be the focus of the paper, but you still do not have a clear statement that describes the content of your paper. Your thesis statement will explain your argument and will show that you have focused the paper on a limited area appropriate to the assigned word length.

If you were writing a long paper on this topic, you would compose a thesis statement that would allow you to examine one major aspect of this topic. For example, your thesis could be

> The relationship between money and motivation is demonstrated in salary negotiation demands found in both business and industry.

You have explained the focus of your paper, and you have outlined the approach you will take.

Your thesis would have to be more specific if you were assigned a shorter paper on this topic. In a short paper, you would not have room to launch into a lengthy discussion. An appropriate thesis for a short paper could be

> The main factor motivating police officers to accept overtime assignments is money.

By looking at these thesis statements, you can see that the same topic could be approached in different ways depending on the length of the paper. Once your position on the topic is presented, devote the rest of the research paper to proving that this position is correct.

You should incorporate your thesis into the first paragraph of your paper. Some writers like to use the thesis as the first sentence. This is a good place for the thesis, particularly if you have trouble writing opening paragraphs. Other writers prefer to use several interesting "attention-getting" sentences at the beginning and then to present the thesis as the last sentence of the opening paragraph. Placing the thesis in the first paragraph gives the reader a blueprint for the argument that will be developed in the remainder of the paper.

(c) Step 3: Research

The research paper is, by nature, an investigation of the topic assigned. To complete this investigation, you need to collect all of the information available on that topic, sort out what is useful, and present an argument supported by this information.

Information can be collected in several ways. One way is to do primary research. You could conduct a survey and analyze the results, or you could interview experts on the topic. This method yields original and interesting information, but there are disadvantages. Primary research requires more time than other methods, and you need good statistical, survey designing, and interview skills to ensure that your research is valid. For these reasons, most writers turn to secondary research for information.

A good library will give you the opportunity to investigate your topic by reading what other researchers have already discovered. Follow the guide listed below to acquaint yourself with the facilities of the library you are using.

1. Search for entries under your topic in the computerized catalogue of the library system. With most libraries using automated catalogues, you can conduct your search using computer terminals located in the particular library branch. The catalogues are typically accessed using the title of the work or the author's name, or subject headings or key words in the subject heading. If you are trying to find information for a paper on management theories, search the entries under the subject heading "management". Don't limit yourself to the topic itself. Look under subject headings that could be related to your topic. As "managment" is a very broad subject, the catalogue will often provide cross-references to more focused subheadings. For example, there may be cross-references to "office management", "organizational behaviour" or "personnel management".

   For each entry listed, you can obtain details of the format of the work, the author, the title, the publisher and date of publication, the number of pages, the main subjects covered, and the ISBN number. Where your search is conducted in a multi-branch library system, a further feature provided is the availability of the work in the different branches, the number of copies, the catalogue number, and whether it is in the reference section or on an open shelf.

2. Search the online indexes of periodicals available through the library system. Using the computer terminals at the particular branch, you can conduct searches using the automated indexes of articles in magazines, newspapers and other periodicals. Some indexes such as the Expanded Academic ASAP contain the full text of certain articles, or an abstract of the article or an extended citation. With some library systems, a library card holder can have the text of these articles emailed to the card holder's email address at no charge. For indexes of exclusively Canadian materials, there is Electric Library Canada, and the Canadian Periodical Index. In addition, there is the paper version of the Canadian Periodical Index or the Index to Canadian Legal Literature, and the volumes of the Reader's Guide to Periodical Literature.

   The indexes organize the magazine and newspaper articles into categories using Library of Congress subject headings. By searching under a subject heading or using keywords, a listing of entries of the relevant articles is derived. With this information, you can search the automated library catalogue to find the location of the periodical on the library shelves or whether the article is available on microfiche, as is the case with older articles.

3. Some libraries also contain a collection of newspaper clippings called a "Vertical File" to support certain collections such as Canadian artists or personalities. However, with the extensive indexing of Canadian periodicals, they have been largely replaced by the online databases.

4. Encyclopedias, business indexes, and other reference works are located in the reference section of the library. Encyclopedias can provide a good general introduction to your topic. Other reference works will provide statistics and more specific information that can be extremely helpful when you develop support for your thesis. Most general reference works are available on the open shelves of the main reference area but some materials are in the enclosed stacks and must be retrieved by the library staff.

5. Libraries also contain information in the form of audiotapes, records, films, and videotapes. Explore these sources too. For example, viewing a relevant video might give you insight into the subject of your paper.

6. The internet also provides a valuable source of information. Again, search by related topics but limit your field of the search so you keep your research on topic.

After you have located information that you feel might be useful, gather that information and sort it. Use the tables of contents and indexes in books to find appropriate sections. Scan the sections quickly, and return books that prove to be irrelevant to your topic. As you read, try to follow the author's argument, and watch for quotations that could be used to back up your own observations.

To complete your research as quickly as possible, take notes as you read. As you take research notes, devise a method of noting quotations taken directly from the books, sections you have summarized in your own words, and original ideas that have occurred to you during your research. You could colour-code your entries using blue for quotations, red for summaries, and pencil for your own ideas. If this is too awkward, you could put codes in the margin of your notes adjacent to the various entries, such as "Q" for quotations, "S" for summaries, and asterisks ("*") for your own ideas. Whichever method you choose, make sure that you note the page numbers for quotations and summaries. These page numbers will be needed later for documentation. Some writers like to keep notes from each source on a separate sheet. At the top of the sheet, they record the name of the book, the author's name, the publisher, the city of publication, and the date of publication. This information will be needed in your research paper when you document your sources.

(d) Step 4: Organize Your Information

When you have completed your research, organize your research notes. Check the information in your notes against your thesis statement. Have you stayed on topic or have you wandered into other areas? Decide whether the information you have found can be organized into a logical pattern that you could use in your essay. Arrange your notes so that you will be able to find what you need when you need it.

Finally, re-evaluate your thesis. You might have found some information that will force you to revise your thesis or limit it further. Perhaps you have not found enough information on the topic and should expand your research.

(e) Step 5: Determine Your Audience

Who is going to read your paper? The answer to this question will determine the tone and the content of your paper. If your reader is a professor, you can presume that he or she has some knowledge of the topic you are pursuing, but will need a well-defined thesis to show what aspect of that topic you have investigated. Your tone will have to be clear and precise, with a well-developed and controlled vocabulary. In short, an academic research paper is a serious intellectual argument in which you present a thesis and defend it.

If you are writing a promotional essay, the tone must still be controlled and correct, but the purpose of this type of essay is different.

The person reading your essay will be looking for a demonstration of your understanding of the theoretical aspect of your topic. He or she will be assessing your ability to apply this theory to a specific area. This reflects skills of organization and application of information, qualities that would be essential for a senior ranking officer.

No matter which type of paper you are writing, avoid trying to guess what the reader would "like" in a subjective or personal way. The reader will want to read a good paper. It is as simple as that. However, the reader will not be able to "read between the lines" or guess what you were trying to say. Develop your argument clearly, completely, and logically.

(f) Step 6: Write the Outline

The outline serves as a map for your research paper; without a good map you could lose your way. The outline will give you the chance to edit and make changes before you invest too much time in writing.

An outline should be a point-form diagram of the structure of your paper. Look at the outline plan for research papers given below. It shows the organizational pattern you should use for your paper. List each main point that you plan to include in your paper. For each main point, list the evidence you will use to prove that it is correct.

A WORKING OUTLINE PLAN

1st Section:

Opening Sentence(s):________________________________

____

Thesis Statement:__________________________________

____

General Observation(s) or Explanation(s):_______________

____

2nd Section:

First Main Point___________________________________

____

Support/ Evidence_________________________________

____

3rd Section:

Second Main Point______________________________

____

Support/ Evidence______________________________

____

4th Section:

Third Main Point_______________________________

____

Support/ Evidence______________________________

____

Final Section:

Conclusion:__________________________________

Summary of Most Important Idea___________________

____

Recommendations or Application of Information__________

____

As soon as you have completed the outline, check the information you have included. If there are flaws in the outline itself, these flaws will be duplicated in the paper. Ask yourself these questions:

1. Are all of the major points in the outline relevant to the thesis?
2. Is the outline well organized, with each point leading logically to the next point?
3. Is each point adequately supported? Vague generalizations will not develop your argument.
4. Should more material be included? Refer to your research notes.
5. Have you relied too heavily on your sources and failed to add your own observations or analysis? After all, it is your paper and should reflect your thoughts on the subject.

(g) Step 7: Write a Draft

From your outline, you can see the sections of the paper and each point you are going to discuss. Now develop these points in complete sentences and well-developed paragraphs. Each paragraph should contain only one fully developed idea. Paragraphs containing many different ideas make your discussion confusing. Also, avoid one-sentence paragraphs; it is difficult to develop an idea fully in only one sentence.

When you write your paper, it is acceptable to use the ideas or words of others if you give full credit to the sources of that information. This allows you to present your own ideas and support them with the information from your research. Documentation of the source material is discussed in detail in Chapter 10. Refer to it to determine the correct format for your parenthetical references and Works Cited list.

When you are writing the draft of the paper, do not become discouraged if a paragraph or even an entire section does not satisfy you. Plod along and keep writing. You are not trying to complete a final version of the paper at this early stage. After you have completed the first draft, you can revise what you have written. If you are typing rather than working on a computer, double or triple space your paper so that you have room for your revisions. It is much easier to revise words on paper than to revise ideas that are still in your head.

You do not have to complete the entire draft in one sitting either. Your outline shows the sections that you must complete, but you do not have to complete them in the order in which they are listed. If writing an introduction is difficult for you, complete the body of the paper before writing the introduction. The sections can be rearranged after they have been completed.

After you have completed the first draft of the paper, leave it for a while. The paper will be easier to revise and edit and you will be able to read it more objectively after it has "cooled off".

(h) Step 8: Revise and Edit

Revising and editing are the most important steps in the writing process. Although all of the required ideas may have been included in the paper, it is not complete until those ideas have been expressed clearly and correctly. The first draft is not "carved in stone" and may be altered. In fact, the first draft often bears little resemblance to the final version of the paper. The first draft is only the raw material in the process of writing.

To begin this step in the writing process, read the paper to get an overview of it, and then examine the following areas:

1. **Does the discussion stay within the bounds established by the thesis?**

   Including everything you know about the topic might be impressive, but this is not the purpose of the paper. Check all of the information to make sure it is relevant to the specific area defined by the thesis.

2. **Is the organization of the material effective or should it he rearranged?**

   Use the thesis to help you to find an effective organizational pattern. By breaking the thesis into units of thought, you can see the order in which information should be discussed.

3. **Is the paper complete?**

   Anticipate all of the questions which your reader could ask, and then include the answers to these questions within the discussion you have presented.

4. **Have you presumed too much knowledge on the part of the reader?**

   Assume that your reader is an intelligent person interested in your discussion, but do not reference information or background knowledge that the reader needs to understand your argument unless you provide this information.

5. **Does your paper have a clear beginning, middle, and end?**

   Your reader should feel comfortable with the flow of information presented. If the paper begins without an introduction, the reader will react with surprise. If the paper does not have a definite body, the reader will presume that you have nothing to say. If the paper does not have a conclusion, the reader will feel as though the paper is incomplete.

After you have completed the above steps, improve the way that you have expressed your ideas. Again, start on the large areas and work down to the details. Use the following guidelines:

1. **Is all of the information within each paragraph focused on one main idea?**

   If you include too many ideas within one paragraph, your writing will appear disorganized.

2. **Are the paragraphs linked so that your writing is coherent?**

   Add transitional words or phrases to give your writing a natural flow.

3. **Is each sentence effectively worded?**

   Rearranging the word order, changing the word choice and improving the structure of the sentences will strengthen your paper.

4. **Have you varied the lengths of the sentences?**

   It is easy to fall into the trap of writing sentences that are all of equal length. This makes your writing dull.

5. **Is each word the correct and most accurate word choice?**

   Check the correct meaning of words by using a dictionary or a thesaurus to find a word that may be more appropriate. Avoid unnecessary repetition of specific words.

Finally, turn your attention to the mechanics of writing. Check for the following:

1. **Spelling**

   Get out your dictionary and look up any words that you think might be misspelled, or use your computer spell check program.

2. **Punctuation**

   Sentences that are not punctuated properly could confuse your reader.

3. **Grammar**

   Grammatical errors can cause confusion, and they reveal a lack of attention to detail. As a result, your reader is forced to edit rather than simply to follow the discussion you have presented.

The editing and re-writing process should be repeated several times until you are satisfied with the final product. When you are satisfied, prepare a final copy of your paper for submission.

(i) Step 9: Prepare the Final Copy

You have likely heard the old saying "Don't judge a book by its cover." While this might be a good saying, it is not very realistic. Everyone makes judgments based on appearances, and readers of research papers are no exception. If you present a paper that looks like trash, readers will assume that it *is* trash. Assume that your paper is a product which you must sell. In order for it to sell, it must be packaged in an attractive manner.

Advertisers use this technique, and it would be wise to take a moment to examine why it is successful. Imagine, for a moment, that you have come up with a scheme to save a cereal company millions of dollars. You argue that, instead of spending all of their money on new packages for the cereal, they could recycle the old boxes. Since the product in the box is protected by a new waxed paper wrapper, the appearance of the box should not matter to the consumer. Your idea is accepted, and soon your company offers the cereal to the public in old, torn, used boxes. Does the scheme save money? No. The people who had been buying that brand switch to another brand which comes packaged in new boxes. Why do they switch when the quality of the cereal in the old box has not changed? Quite simply, the appearance of the product is not attractive.

The content of your paper is like the cereal in the box. Even if it is a quality product, it must have an attractive appearance if you want to influence your reader in a positive way. You want to impress your reader with the quality of the presentation as well as with the quality of the content.

Papers must be typed (or computer printed), not handwritten.

Just as you would not want to read books or articles handwritten by the author, your reader will not want to read a handwritten paper. Your handwriting might be neat and legible, but it will never be as easy to read or look as business-like as a typed copy. Type or print (from the computer) your paper on good quality white paper, leaving adequate margins of approximately $1\frac{1}{2}$ inches or 40 millimetres on the sides, top, and bottom. Staple the paper in the upper left hand corner, include a title page, and arrange pages in the correct order.

Follow all of the directions you were given about title pages, binding or stapling, and margin sizes. Many departments or professors issue a page of directions for the format of research papers. Papers that do not conform to these requirements annoy the reader and, in some cases, may be rejected before they are read.

Your presentation should reflect your professional standards. If the paper looks like an "amateur production", it weakens the image you are attempting to portray and undermines the information.

(j) Step 10: Proofread

Do not try to proofread your paper immediately after it has been written. Wait at least a few hours so that you will be able to see exactly what you wrote instead of what you intended to write. Recognize that you will have to read through the paper several times to catch all of the errors. Of course, the pages with errors should be retyped or reprinted.

Learning how to catch errors requires patience and practice.

When proofreading, check the accuracy of the typing, the punctuation of the sentences, and the spelling of the words. However, do not become distracted by the ideas in the paper. Look at each sentence separately and analytically; then, check the words within the sentence. Some writers find it effective to proofread their papers in reverse from the last sentence to the first sentence so that the content becomes secondary to the structure of the sentences. Other writers place a blank sheet of paper over the typed pages and reveal one line at a time. This prevents your eyes from racing from one line to the next. Another useful method of proofreading is reading the paper out loud. This helps to check whether the sentences you have written sound correct. In addition to this, get someone else to proofread your essay. Another person can bring a fresh perspective to what you have written and may spot errors you did not notice.

10

Documentation

The research you do makes you more informed about your topic and provides the evidence you will need to convince the reader that your thesis is correct. When you write your research paper, you must clearly distinguish your ideas and words from the ideas and words of your sources. If you do not make this distinction, you could be accused of plagiarism.

Plagiarism is theft. If you do not credit your sources for their ideas and words, you are stealing information and claiming it as your own. Remember that the purpose of the research paper is to give you the opportunity to learn and to present your ideas and observations on the assigned topic. Source material can be used to support your ideas, but it cannot be used as a substitute for your ideas.

In order to avoid being accused of plagiarism, you must document your sources. There are different systems of documentation. The American Psychological Association (APA) and the Modern Languages Association (MLA) are two of the most commonly used systems of documentation. The APA style of documentation is often used for social sciences papers, and the MLA style of documentation is often used for humanities papers. If you are not sure which system to use, check with your instructor. Each system has slight variations in the way works are listed. Once you have decided which system you are going to use, it is crucial that you follow the format exactly.

In 1984 the MLA adopted a system that, like the APA style, uses parenthetical references in the text instead of footnotes. Footnotes are now used only to give additional explanations or supplementary information.

The list of sources given at the end of the paper is called the "Works Cited" list. This differs slightly from a bibliography. While a bibliography is a general list of works related to one topic, the Works Cited list gives only the sources that were referred to in the body of the paper. Some instructors prefer a bibliography with the research paper; other instructors prefer a Works Cited list. Check with your instructor for specific directions.

1. APA STYLE

(a) Using APA Style References within the Paper

The APA style of documentation uses parenthetical references within the research paper to identify sources. Whenever an idea or a quotation from a source is used, the source is identified for the reader. Enough information is given in the parenthetical reference to allow the reader to check the Works Cited list at the end of the paper for a complete reference of the source.

When giving references within the paper in APA style, follow these guidelines:

1. Whenever you refer to a source, give the author's name and the date of the publication. If the author's name is already mentioned in the sentence, just give the date of publication in the parentheses. For example,

    > Millard (1985) examines the need for legal protection of computer programs and data.

    If the author's name is not included in the sentence, give both the author's name and the date of publication in the parentheses. For example,

    > Computer programs and data need legal protection (Millard, 1985).

    Notice that the period follows the parenthetical reference.

2. If the work being described has two authors, give both of the names.

(In APA style, up to six authors are all listed in the reference. If the work has more than six authors, then the term "et al." is used to indicate "and others".)

If the names are given in the sentence, join them with the word "and". If they are given in the parentheses, join the names with the ampersand symbol. For example,

> Kerr and King (1998) describe the structure and operation of organizations and the rules of order by which organizations function.
>
> Or
>
> It is essential to understand the structure and operation of organizations and the rules of order by which organizations function (Kerr & King, 1998).

3. When a direct quotation is taken from a source, include the page number in the parenthetical reference. For example,

> Salhany (1986) observes, "Police duties and powers will not be extended to the enforcement of non-existent laws or extend to actions taken in ignorance of the law" (p. 17).
>
> Or
>
> "Police duties and powers will not be extended to the enforcement of non-existent laws or extend to actions taken in ignorance of the law" (Salhany, 1986, p. 17).

For electronic sources, use a paragraph number if available, using either the "¶" symbol or "para." If the paragraphs are unnumbered, refer to a heading if available and the relevant number of the paragraph following it. For example,

> Salhany (1986) observes, "Police duties and powers will not be extended to the enforcement of non-existent laws or extend to actions taken in ignorance of the law" (¶ 17).
>
> Or
>
> "Police duties and powers will not be extended to the enforcement of non-existent laws or extend to actions taken in ignorance of the law" (Salhany, 1986, Introduction section, para. 3).

4. References to personal communications, such as letters, memos, emails, or interviews, are included as parenthetical references in the text. However, in APA style these references are not listed in the Works Cited because the reader cannot get access to the original work. For example,

   Eric Elstone (personal interview, July 15, 2002) explained that the press must have access to court documents.

5. If a long quotation (over 40 words) is included in the research paper, the quotation is indented .5 inch, 1.3 cm, or five spaces from the left margin. The quotation is double spaced like the rest of the research paper. No quotation marks are used if the quotation is indented, and the end punctuation is placed before the parenthetical page references. For example,

   In *Understanding Criminal Offences,* Saxton and Stansfield (1987) observe:

   > The proof of conspiracy is often a very difficult matter, particularly if the *actus reus* was merely a verbal agreement, as is usual. How can you prove a conversation took place, let alone what was said? Typically, conspiracy charges are proven by one of the conspirators providing a statement or confession incriminating his co-conspirators. (p. 235)

6. If you want to refer to a source that has been quoted in one of the sources you have read, use a secondary citation. For example,

   The Canadian Law Dictionary defines conspiracy as an "agreement between two or more persons to do an act that is unlawful or a lawful act by unlawful means" (cited in Saxton & Stansfield, 1987, p. 235).

(b) APA Style: Works Cited List

The Works Cited list always starts on a separate page at the end of the paper. Entries are not numbered, but they are listed alphabetically according to the author's last name.

There are several other characteristics of the Works Cited list in APA style. These include the following:

1. Authors' initials rather than first names are used.
2. Capitals are only used for the first word, or proper names, in titles.
3. The date of publication is placed in parentheses.
4. Entries are double spaced. The first line of an entry begins at the left margin. Subsequent lines are indented three spaces.
5. Titles of works are underlined *or* put in italics.

The following guideline provides samples of the way different types of works are listed in the Works Cited according to APA style:

One Author

Holland, W. (1998). *The Law of Theft and Related Offences.* Toronto: Carswell.

Two Authors

Morton, J.C., & Hutchison, S. (1987). *The presumption of innocence.* Toronto: Carswell.

Three Authors

Krivel, E.F., Beveridge, T. & Hayward, J.W. (2002). *A Practical Guide to Canadian Extradition.* Toronto: Carswell.

Corporate Author

Toronto Police Service. (2001). *Annual report 2000.* Toronto: Author.

(Note that when the author and the publisher are the same, the publisher is given as "Author".)

Edition

Pearsall, T.E., Cunningham, D.H., & Smith, E.O. (2000). *How to write for the world of work* (6th ed). New York: Holt, Rinehart and Winston.

Editor

Goepfert, P.S. (Ed.). (1982). *The communications handbook.* Toronto: Nelson.

Work in an Anthology or Collection

Stamler, R.T. (1987). Organized Crime. In R.L. Linden (Ed.), *Criminology: A Canadian perspective* (pp. 270-294). Toronto: Holt, Rinehart and Winston.

Journal or Magazine Article

Witham, D.C., & Field, G. (1988, October). The key to successful management. *Police Chief*, 62-63.

(Note that the volume number, if any, appears in italics following the name of the journal or magazine.)

Unsigned Journal or Magazine Article

Hisses for Hollywood. (1989, June). *Maclean's*, 6.

Newspaper Article

McRae, C. (1989, July 8). More to racing than just driving car. *The Toronto Star*, p. J15.

Secondary Citation (The secondary source is noted in the paper by giving "as cited in". The secondary source, rather than the primary source, is given in the Works Cited list.)

Saxton, B. & Stansfield, R. (1987). *Understanding criminal offences.* Toronto: Carswell.

Electronic Source (For electronic sources such as online periodicals, databases, and websites, set out, for example, the author if any, title of article, title of periodical, volume number, paragraph numbers, date retrieved from source, and the internet address or uniform resource locator (URL) of the source, as in the fictional example below.)

Sugimoto, T. (2002, January 27). Recent amendments to the *Criminal Code. Law Journal, 76*, 19-25. Retrieved July 18, 2002 from http://www.carswell.com/journals/crim/76-1.html

(Note that no period follows the internet address or URL in APA style. If the address continues onto another line, break the line either after a slash or before a period; do not hyphenate.)

For more information about APA style of documentation, refer to

American Psychological Association. (2001). *Publication manual of the American Psychological Association* (5th ed.). Washington, DC: Author.

2. MLA STYLE

(a) Using MLA Style References Within the Paper

When giving references within the research paper in MLA style, use the following guidelines:

1. If the author's name is given in the sentence, no parenthetical reference is needed unless the paper includes references to two works by the same author. For example,

   Reference to one work:

   > Millard believes that computer programs and data need legal protection.

   Reference to two works:

   > Sarna describes current issues in corporate organization in *Corporate Structure, Finance and Operations: Essays on the Law and Business Practice* and discusses contemporary letter of credit transactions in *Letters of Credit: The Law and Current Practice.*
   >
   > Or
   >
   > Sarna describes current issues in corporate organization *(Corporate Structure)* and discusses contemporary letter of credit transactions *(Letters of Credit).*

   Notice that shortened versions of the titles are used in parenthetical references to the work. The complete titles are given in the Works Cited list at the end of the paper.

2. If the work has two or three authors, give all of the names in the parentheses. For example,

   > The basic elements of business law are analyzed from two perspectives (Simmonds, Smith, and Mercer 417-48).

   If the work has more than three authors, give the name of the first author listed in the Works Cited list followed by the term "et al." For example,

   > Family law precedents and the preparation of domestic documents are also discussed (MacDonald et al.).

(Alternatively, all of the last names can be given. Ensure, however, that the format in the text matches that of the entry in Works Cited.)

3. For direct quotations, give both the author's name and the page number. For example,

> Salhany observes, "Police duties and powers will not be extended to the enforcement of non-existent laws or extend to actions taken in ignorance of the law" (17).
>
> Or
>
> "Police duties and powers will not be extended to the enforcement of non-existent laws or extend to actions taken in ignorance of the law" (Salhany 17).

Notice that the author's name and the page number are not separated by a comma.

For electronic sources, cite a paragraph number if available, using "par." or "pars." For example,

> Salhany observes, "Police duties and powers will not be extended to the enforcement of non-existent laws or extend to actions taken in ignorance of the law" (pars. 17-18).

4. References to personal communications, such as letters, memos, emails, or interviews, are included in parenthetical references in the text. In MLA style, they are also listed in the Works Cited list. For example,

> Eric Elstone (letter, 15 July 2002) explained that the press must have access to court documents.

5. If you include a long quotation (over four typed lines), indent the quotation an additional one inch or ten spaces from the left margin. The quotation is double spaced like the rest of the research paper. No quotation marks are used if the quotation is indented, and the end punctuation is placed before the parenthetical page reference. For example,

> Saxton and Stansfield observe:
>
> > Many of the nefarious ways in which criminals have attempted to exploit the monetary system in the past have to

> some extent been circumvented in practical ways. For example, Canadian bank notes are multicoloured, which makes them extremely difficult to counterfeit. U.S. notes, on the other hand, are green and black, which makes them easier to reproduce. (305)

(b) MLA Style: Works Cited List

The Works Cited list always starts on a separate page at the end of the paper. Entries are not numbered, but are listed alphabetically according to the author's last name.

There are several other characteristics of the Works Cited list written in MLA style. These include the following:

1. Authors' full names are included.
2. All major words in titles are capitalized.
3. Entries are double spaced. The first line of an entry begins at the left margin. Subsequent lines are indented .5 inch from the left margin or five spaces.
4. The date follows the publisher's name.
5. Titles of works are underlined *or* put in italics.

The following guideline provides samples of the way different types of sources are listed in the Works Cited according to MLA style:

One Author

> Holland, Winifred. *The Law of Theft and Related Offences.* Toronto: Carswell, 1998.

Two or Three Authors

> Krivel, Elaine F., Thomas Beveridge, and John W. Hayward. *A Practical Guide to Canadian Extradition.* Toronto: Carswell, 2002.

More Than Three Authors

> Meehan, Eugene, et al. *The 1999 Annotated Canadian Charter of Rights and Freedoms.* Toronto: Carswell, 1998.

Or

> Meehan, Eugene, Karen M. Cuddy, Clive Elkin, H. Scott Fairley, Norm Fera, Ronald Martland, Michael S. Rankin, John D. Richard, and J. David Wake. *The 1999 Annotated Canadian Charter of Rights and Freedoms.* Toronto: Carswell, 1998.

Corporate Author

Toronto Police Service. *Annual Report 2000.* Toronto: Toronto Police Service, 2001.

Edition

Pearsall, Thomas E., David H. Cunningham, and Elizabeth O. Smith. *How to Write for the World of Work.* 6th ed. New York: Holt, Rinehart and Winston, 2000.

Editor

Goepfert, Paula S., ed. *The Communications Handbook.* Toronto: Nelson, 1982.

Work in an Anthology or Collection

Stamler, Rodney T., "Organized Crime." *Criminology: A Canadian Perspective.* Ed. Rick Linden. Toronto: Holt, Rinehart and Winston, 1987. 270-94.

Journal or Magazine Article

Witham, Donald C. and Ginny Field. "The Key to Successful Management." *Police Chief*, 17 (Oct. 1988): 62-63.

(Note that the volume number, if any, appears following the name of the journal or magazine.)

Unsigned Journal or Magazine Article

"Hisses for Hollywood." *Maclean's* June 1989: 6.

Newspaper Article

McRae, Cam. "More to Racing than Just Driving Car." *Toronto Star* 8 July 1989, final ed.: J 15.

Personal Communication

Elstone, Eric. Letter to the author. 15 July 2002.

Electronic Source (Electronic sources include online periodicals, databases, websites, etc. For a database, list the name of the database, editor if any, version or date of the update, sponsoring organization, date of access and retrieval address, as in the fictional example below.)

Criminal Code Project. Ed. T. Sugimoto. January 2002. Criminal Code Association. 1 April 2002. <http://www.crimcodeassn.org/ccp/updatejan02.html>

(Note that if the internet address continues onto another line, break the line either after a slash or before a period; do not hyphenate.)

For further information about MLA style of documentation, refer to

Gibaldi, Joseph. *MLA Handbook for Writers of Research Papers.* (5th ed.). New York: Modern Languages Association, 1999.

Appendix

Sample Police Report Forms*

- Address Report
- Aircraft Report
- Alcohol Report
- Arrest Report
- Bicycle Report
- Boat Motor Report
- Business/Organization Report
- Criminal Organization Report
- Drugs Report
- Firearm Report
- Fraudulent Document Report
- General Occurrence Report
- General Property Report
- Involved Person Report
- Missing Person Report
- Notes Report
- Police Document Report
- Police Investigative Tool Report
- Security Report
- Sudden Death/Homicide Report
- Supplementary Report
- Vehicle Report
- Victim's Report
- Watercraft Report
- Additional Narrative

---

* Reproduced with permission. These sample police report forms were provided by Inspector Robert Dymock, St. Thomas Police Service, Ontario. Please see Part One of this book on police reports.

Address Report Occurrence # Badge #

Classification (Select all that apply)

☐ Arrested
☐ Accused
☐ Attending Physician
☐ Charged
☐ Complainant
☐ Coroner
☐ Cyclist
☐ Deceased
☐ Escapee
☐ Finder
☐ Located
☐ Missing
☐ NOK
☐ Owner
☐ Pedestrian
☐ Reporter
☐ Suicidal
☐ Suspect
☐ Vehicle driver
☐ Vehicle passenger
☐ Victim(crime person)
☐ Victim(property crime)
☐ Victim(OMPPAC)
☐ Wanted
☐ Warned
☐ Witness
☐ YO under 16
☐ YO 16-17 crim. offence
☐ Child under 12
☐ Other

Verified (Select all that apply)

☐ Source: Accused
☐ Source: Complainant
☐ Source: Witness
☐ Source: Informant
☐ Police occurrence
☐ Police street check
☐ Police custody
☐ Police records
☐ Police investigation
☐ Police CAD
☐ CPIC
☐ Birth certificate
☐ SIN card
☐ Photo ID
☐ Other ______________

Address Type: ☐Residence ☐Seasonal ☐Temporary ☐Business ☐NFA ☐Frequents ☐Observed ☐Other

Effective to date: ______________ Include address in Crown brief? (Y/N): ______

Verified how (use above) ______________

St/Fire # ________ Street: ______________ Type: ______ Dir: _____

Mun./Twp: ______________ Region: ________ Prov./State: ______

Postal Code: __________ Country: __________ ☐Apt ☐Suite ☐Unit: _____

Common Name: ______________ Zone: ________

Building details: Floor/Seg.: ______ ______ Room: ________

Building: __________ Complex: ______________

Rural Details: Lot #: ________ Con #: ________ Site #: ________

Mailing address details: Box: ________ Route: ________ Postal district: ________

UCR Type:

☐Unknown
☐Single Home
☐Private property
☐Apartment
☐Hotel
☐Car dealership
☐Financial institution
☐Convenience store
☐Gas station
☐Supervised school
☐Unsupervised school
☐College
☐Parking lots
☐Street or highway
☐Open areas
☐Bus or Bus shelter
☐Other non-commercial place
☐Other commercial place
☐Other public transportation
☐Subway or subway station

Aircraft Report

Occurrence # ______ **Badge #** ______

Classification (Select all that apply)**

- ☐ Abandoned
- ☐ Crime
- ☐ Damaged
- ☐ Involved in Accident
- ☐ Found
- ☐ Held
- ☐ Lost
- ☐ Outstanding
- ☐ Recovered
- ☐ Released
- ☐ Repossessed
- ☐ Seized
- ☐ Stolen
- ☐ Street Check
- ☐ Suspect
- ☐ Towed
- ☐ Other
- ☐ Doors Locked
- ☐ Keys in Vehicle

Verified (Select all that apply)**

- ☐ Source: Accused
- ☐ Source: Complainant
- ☐ Source: Witness
- ☐ Source: Informant
- ☐ Police occurrence
- ☐ Police street check
- ☐ Police custody
- ☐ Police records
- ☐ Police investigation
- ☐ Police CAD
- ☐ CPIC
- ☐ Birth certificate
- ☐ SIN card
- ☐ Photo ID
- ☐ Other ______

Recovery (Select one)

- ☐ Not applicable
- ☐ Not recovered
- ☐ No damage
- ☐ Parts missing
- ☐ Damaged
- ☐ Destroyed-not burned
- ☐ Destroyed-burned
- ☐ Condition unknown

Type (Select one)**

- ☐ Aircraft, general
- ☐ Balloon
- ☐ Glider
- ☐ **Helicopter**
- ☐ Jet plane
- ☐ Jumbo jet plane
- ☐ Light plane
- ☐ Military plane
- ☐ Seaplane
- ☐ Ultra-light plane
- ☐ Propeller plane
- ☐ Turboprop plane
- ☐ Other

Make: ______ **Model:** ______ **Year:** ______

Manufacture Date: ______ **Serial #:** ______

Original Colours: ______/______ **Repainted Colours:** ______/______

Original Value:** ______ **Current Value:**** ______

Common name: ______

Licence #: ______ **Prov/state:** ______

Remarks: ______

Relate to person/business: ______ **DOB:** ______

Involvement (Select one)

- ☐ Driver
- ☐ Finder
- ☐ Leases
- ☐ Owner
- ☐ Passenger
- ☐ Renter
- ☐ Seized from
- ☐ Appraiser
- ☐ Document owner
- ☐ Document owner
- ☐ Document Issuer

Alcohol Report

Occurrence # **Badge #**

Classification (Select all that apply)**

☐ Commercial
☐ Counterfeit
☐ Evidence
☐ Found
☐ Fraud
☐ Held
☐ Lost
☐ Outstanding
☐ Pawned
☐ Proceeds of crime
☐ Prohibited
☐ Recovered
☐ Restricted
☐ Safekeeping
☐ Seized
☐ Stolen
☐ Used in crime
☐ Used as weapon
☐ Other

Verified (Select all that apply)**

☐ Source: Accused
☐ Source: Complainant
☐ Source: Witness
☐ Source: Informant
☐ Police occurrence
☐ Police street check
☐ Police custody
☐ Police records
☐ Police investigation
☐ Police CAD
☐ CPIC
☐ Birth certificate
☐ SIN card
☐ Photo ID
☐ Other ______

Alcohol Type (Select one)**

☐ Beer ☐ Wine ☐ Spirits ☐ Other

Common Name: ______

Brand: ______ **Value:** ______ **Full:** ______ **Partial:** ______

Remarks: ______

Classification (Select all that apply)**

☐ Commercial
☐ Counterfeit
☐ Evidence
☐ Found
☐ Fraud
☐ Held
☐ Lost
☐ Outstanding
☐ Pawned
☐ Proceeds of crime
☐ Prohibited
☐ Recovered
☐ Restricted
☐ Safekeeping
☐ Seized
☐ Stolen
☐ Used in crime
☐ Used as weapon
☐ Other

Verified (Select all that apply)**

☐ Source: Accused
☐ Source: Complainant
☐ Source: Witness
☐ Source: Informant
☐ Police occurrence
☐ Police street check
☐ Police custody
☐ Police records
☐ Police investigation
☐ Police CAD
☐ CPIC
☐ Birth certificate
☐ SIN card
☐ Photo ID
☐ Other ______

Alcohol Type (Select one)**

☐ Beer ☐ Wine ☐ Spirits ☐ Other

Common Name: ______

Brand: ______ **Value:** ______ **Full:** ______ **Partial:** ______

Remarks: ______

Relate to person/business: ______ **DOB:** ______

Involvement (Select one)

☐ Driver
☐ Finder
☐ Leases
☐ Owner
☐ Passenger
☐ Renter
☐ Seized from
☐ Appraiser
☐ Document owner
☐ Document owner
☐ Document Issuer

Arrest Report **Occurrence #** ____________ **Badge #** ____________

Report Date & Time: ____________

Arrested: ____________ DOB: ____________

Arrest Date & Time: ____________ **Arrest Address:** ____________

Arresting Officer(s): ____________ & ____________

Arrest type (Select one)

- ☐ Bench Warrant
- ☐ Committal Warrant
- ☐ Found committing
- ☐ Warrant first Instance
- ☐ Distress
- ☐ Family Court
- ☐ Mental Health Act
- ☐ Reasonable grounds
- ☐ Other

Warrant #: ____________ **Release Date & Time:** ____________

Release Method (Select one)

- ☐ Appearance notice
- ☐ Promise to appear
- ☐ Recognizance OIC w/surety
- ☐ Recognizance OIC wo/surety
- ☐ Recognizance POA form 134
- ☐ Unconditional
- ☐ Undertaking OIC w/wo conditions
- ☐ Undertaking Judge/Justice w/wo conditions
- ☐ Undertaking – responsible person
- ☐ YO Appearance notice
- ☐ YO Promise to appear
- ☐ YO order- judge or justice
- ☐ YO Undertaking w/wo conditions
- ☐ Other

Releasing Officer: ____________ **Fingerprint Date:** ____________

Personal Effects/Money

Locker/Bag #: ____________ **Cash taken (amount):** ____________ **Taken by Badge #:** ____________

Property Description: ____________

____

Property taken by Officer #: ____________

Arrest Narrative:

____

____

____

____

____

____

____

____

____

Continue on back

Bicycle Report **Occurrence #** **Badge #**

Classification (Select all that apply) **

☐ Commercial ☐ Counterfeit ☐ Evidence ☐ Found ☐ Fraud
☐ Held ☐ Lost ☐ Outstanding ☐ Pawned ☐ Proceeds of crime
☐ Prohibited ☐ Recovered ☐ Restricted ☐ Safekeeping ☐ Seized
☐ Stolen ☐ Used in crime ☐ Used as weapon ☐ Other

Verified (Select all that apply) **

☐ Source: Accused ☐ Source: Complainant ☐ Source: Witness ☐ Source: Informant
☐ Police occurrence ☐ Police street check ☐ Police custody ☐ Police records
☐ Police investigation ☐ Police CAD ☐ CPIC ☐ Birth certificate
☐ SIN card ☐ Photo ID ☐ Other ______

Type (Select one)

☐ Antique ☐ BMX ☐ Cross country ☐ Downhill ☐ Dual Slalom
☐ Freestyle ☐ Folding ☐ Mountain ☐ Racing ☐ Recumbent
☐ Regular ☐ Sidewalk ☐ Tandem ☐ Touring
☐ Tricycle-adult ☐ Tricycle-child ☐ Unicycle ☐ Other

Make: ______ **Model:** ______ **Year:** ______

Manufacture Date: ______ **Serial #:** ______ **Aux. Serial #:** ______

Original Colours: ______/______ **Repainted Colours:** ______/______

Original Value **: ______ **Current Value **:** ______ **Wheels:** ______ **Speeds:** ______

Frame (Select one)

☐ Female ☐ Folding ☐ Male ☐ Unisex ☐ Other

Frame Size (Select one)

☐ Adult ☐ Youth ☐ Child ☐ Other

Handlebars (Select one)

☐ Bullhorn ☐ Racing ☐ Downhill ☐ Other ☐ Highrise ☐ Monkey ☐ Mountain

Seat Style (Select one)

☐ Banana ☐ Regular ☐ Female custom ☐ Others ☐ Gel ☐ Male custom ☐ Racing

Parts (Select that all apply)

☐ Air Pump ☐ Basket ☐ Bell ☐ Carrier
☐ Coaster ☐ Computer ☐ Fenders ☐ Foot straps
☐ Fork shocks ☐ Frame pouch ☐ Helmet ☐ Kickstand
☐ Light ☐ Mirror ☐ Saddlebags ☐ Training wheels
☐ Trip meter ☐ Water bottle ☐ Horn

Remarks: ______

Relate to person/business: ______ **DOB:** ______

Involvement (Select one)

☐ Driver ☐ Finder ☐ Leases
☐ Owner ☐ Passenger ☐ Renter
☐ Seized from ☐ Appraiser ☐ Document owner
☐ Document owner ☐ Document Issuer

Boat Motor Report **Occurrence #** **Badge #**

Classification (Select all that apply)**

☐ Commercial
☐ Counterfeit
☐ Evidence
☐ Found
☐ Fraud
☐ Held
☐ Lost
☐ Outstanding
☐ Pawned
☐ Proceeds of crime
☐ Prohibited
☐ Recovered
☐ Restricted
☐ Safekeeping
☐ Seized
☐ Stolen
☐ Used in crime
☐ Used as weapon
☐ Other

Verified (Select all that apply)**

☐ Source: Accused
☐ Source: Complainant
☐ Source: Witness
☐ Source: Informant
☐ Police occurrence
☐ Police street check
☐ Police custody
☐ Police records
☐ Police investigation
☐ Police CAD
☐ CPIC
☐ Birth certificate
☐ SIN card
☐ Photo ID
☐ Other ____________

Boat Motor Type (Select one)

☐ Inboard motor(s) ☐ Inboard/ Outboard ☐ Outboard motor(s) ☐ Other

Description (Select one)

☐ **Diesel** ☐ **Electric** ☐ **Gasoline** ☐ **Jet** ☐ **Other**

Make: ____________ **Model:** ____________ **Year:** ________

Manuf. Date: ____________ **Serial#:** ____________ **Aux.Serial #:** ____________

Original Colours: ________/________ **Repainted:** ________/________

Value (original):** ____________ **Value (current):**** ____________ **Horsepower:** ______

Remarks: ____

Relate to person/business: ____________________ **DOB:** ____________

Involvement (Select one)

☐ Driver
☐ Finder
☐ Leases
☐ Owner
☐ Passenger
☐ Renter
☐ Seized from
☐ Appraiser
☐ Document owner
☐ Document owner
☐ Document Issuer

Business/Organization Report **Occurrence #** **Badge #**

Classification (Select all that apply)

- ☐ Arrested
- ☐ Accused
- ☐ Attending Physician
- ☐ Charged
- ☐ Complainant
- ☐ Coroner
- ☐ Cyclist
- ☐ Deceased
- ☐ Escapee
- ☐ Finder
- ☐ Located
- ☐ Missing
- ☐ NOK
- ☐ Owner
- ☐ Pedestrian
- ☐ Reporter
- ☐ Suicidal
- ☐ Suspect
- ☐ Vehicle driver
- ☐ Vehicle passenger
- ☐ Victim(crime person)
- ☐ Victim(property crime)
- ☐ Victim(OMPPAC)
- ☐ Wanted
- ☐ Warned
- ☐ Witness
- ☐ YO under 16
- ☐ YO 16-17 crim. offence
- ☐ Child under 12
- ☐ Other

Verified (Select all that apply)

- ☐ Source: Accused
- ☐ Source: Complainant
- ☐ Source: Witness
- ☐ Source: Informant
- ☐ Police occurrence
- ☐ Police street check
- ☐ Police custody
- ☐ Police records
- ☐ Police investigation
- ☐ Police CAD
- ☐ CPIC
- ☐ Birth certificate
- ☐ SIN card
- ☐ Photo ID
- ☐ Other ____________

Type (Select one)

- ☐ Bar
- ☐ Business
- ☐ Church
- ☐ Communication centre
- ☐ Convenience store
- ☐ Day-care
- ☐ Department store
- ☐ Drug store
- ☐ Factory
- ☐ Fast food
- ☐ Financial institution
- ☐ Fur store
- ☐ Hospital
- ☐ Hotel/motel
- ☐ Institution
- ☐ Institution, public
- ☐ Jail
- ☐ Jewellery store
- ☐ Laundry
- ☐ Liquor/ beer store
- ☐ Manufacturer
- ☐ Restaurant
- ☐ School
- ☐ Service station
- ☐ Store
- ☐ Supermarket
- ☐ Other
- ☐ Unknown

Class (Select one)

- ☐ **Complainant address**
- ☐ **Dispatch address**
- ☐ **Occurrence address**
- ☐ **Crime scene**
- ☐ **Property recovered at**
- ☐ **Property lost at**
- ☐ **Other**

Start date: ____________ **Continued date:** ____________

Remarks: ____________

____

Name: ____________

Name Type (Select one)

☐ **Primary** ☐ **Nickname** ☐ **Variant** ☐ **Acronym** ☐ **Legal** ☐ **Operating**

Relate to person/business: ____________ **DOB:** ____________

Involvement (Select one)

- ☐ Driver
- ☐ Finder
- ☐ Leases
- ☐ Owner
- ☐ Passenger
- ☐ Renter
- ☐ Seized from
- ☐ Appraiser
- ☐ Document owner
- ☐ Document owner
- ☐ Document Issuer

Criminal Organization Report

Occurrence # ____ **Badge #** ____

Classification (Select all that apply)

- ☐ Arrested
- ☐ Accused
- ☐ Attending Physician
- ☐ Charged
- ☐ Complainant
- ☐ Coroner
- ☐ Cyclist
- ☐ Deceased
- ☐ Escapee
- ☐ Finder
- ☐ Located
- ☐ Missing
- ☐ NOK
- ☐ Owner
- ☐ Pedestrian
- ☐ Reporter
- ☐ Suicidal
- ☐ Suspect
- ☐ Vehicle driver
- ☐ Vehicle passenger
- ☐ Victim (crime person)
- ☐ Victim (property crime)
- ☐ Victim (OMPPAC)
- ☐ Wanted
- ☐ Warned
- ☐ Witness
- ☐ YO under 16
- ☐ YO 16-17 crim. offence
- ☐ Child under 12
- ☐ Other

Verified (Select all that apply)

- ☐ Source: Accused
- ☐ Source: Complainant
- ☐ Source: Witness
- ☐ Source: Informant
- ☐ Police occurrence
- ☐ Police street check
- ☐ Police custody
- ☐ Police records
- ☐ Police investigation
- ☐ Police CAD
- ☐ CPIC
- ☐ Birth certificate
- ☐ SIN card
- ☐ Photo ID
- ☐ Other ____

Criminal Organization Type (Select one)

- ☐ Aboriginal organized crime
- ☐ Asian organized crime
- ☐ Eastern European crime
- ☐ Motorcycle gang
- ☐ Russian organized crime
- ☐ Street gang
- ☐ Terrorism
- ☐ Traditional organized crime
- ☐ Other

Class (Select one)

- ☐ Auto theft
- ☐ Extortion
- ☐ Loan sharking
- ☐ Narcotic
- ☐ Prostitution
- ☐ Terrorism
- ☐ Youth
- ☐ Other

Start date: ____ **Discontinued date:** ____

Remarks: ____

____

____

Organization name: ____

Name Type (Select one)

☐ **Primary** ☐ **Nickname** ☐ **Variant** ☐ **Acronym** ☐ **Legal** ☐ **Operating**

Drugs Report **Occurrence #** **Badge #**

Classification (Select all that apply)**

☐ Commercial
☐ Counterfeit
☐ Evidence
☐ Found
☐ Fraud
☐ Held
☐ Lost
☐ Outstanding
☐ Pawned
☐ Proceeds of crime
☐ Prohibited
☐ Recovered
☐ Restricted
☐ Safekeeping
☐ Seized
☐ Stolen
☐ Used in crime
☐ Used as weapon
☐ Other

Verified (Select all that apply)**

☐ Source: Accused
☐ Source: Complainant
☐ Source: Witness
☐ Source: Informant
☐ Police occurrence
☐ Police street check
☐ Police custody
☐ Police records
☐ Police investigation
☐ Police CAD
☐ CPIC
☐ Birth certificate
☐ SIN card
☐ Photo ID
☐ Other ____________

Drug Type (Select one)

☐ Amphetamine
☐ Barbiturates
☐ Crack cocaine
☐ Cocaine
☐ Codeine
☐ Demerol
☐ Dilaudid
☐ Ecstasy
☐ Gamma Hydroxy Butyrate
☐ Halcyon
☐ Hashish
☐ Heroin
☐ Librium
☐ Liquid Hashish
☐ LSD
☐ Magic mushrooms
☐ Marihuana
☐ Marihuana plants
☐ Mescaline
☐ Morphine
☐ Other prescription drugs
☐ Other prohibited drugs
☐ PCP
☐ Percodan
☐ Rohypnol
☐ Talwin
☐ Valium
☐ Other

Value: ____________ **Common name:** ________________________ **Quantity:** ________

Remarks: ____

Classification (Select all that apply)**

☐ Commercial
☐ Counterfeit
☐ Evidence
☐ Found
☐ Fraud
☐ Held
☐ Lost
☐ Outstanding
☐ Pawned
☐ Proceeds of crime
☐ Prohibited
☐ Recovered
☐ Restricted
☐ Safekeeping
☐ Seized
☐ Stolen
☐ Used in crime
☐ Used as weapon
☐ Other

Verified (Select all that apply)**

☐ Source: Accused
☐ Source: Complainant
☐ Source: Witness
☐ Source: Informant
☐ Police occurrence
☐ Police street check
☐ Police custody
☐ Police records
☐ Police investigation
☐ Police CAD
☐ CPIC
☐ Birth certificate
☐ SIN card
☐ Photo ID
☐ Other ____________

Drug Type (Select one)

☐ Amphetamine
☐ Barbiturates
☐ Crack cocaine
☐ Cocaine
☐ Codeine
☐ Demerol
☐ Dilaudid
☐ Ecstasy
☐ Gamma Hydroxy Butyrate
☐ Halcyon
☐ Hashish
☐ Heroin
☐ Librium
☐ Liquid Hashish
☐ LSD
☐ Magic mushrooms
☐ Marihuana
☐ Marihuana plants
☐ Mescaline
☐ Morphine
☐ Other prescription drugs
☐ Other prohibited drugs
☐ PCP
☐ Percodan
☐ Rohypnol
☐ Talwin
☐ Valium
☐ Other

Value: ____________ **Common name:** ________________________ **Quantity:** ________

Remarks: ____

Relate to person/business: ________________________ **DOB:** ____________

Involvement (Select one)

☐ Driver
☐ Finder
☐ Leases
☐ Owner
☐ Passenger
☐ Renter
☐ Seized from
☐ Appraiser
☐ Document owner
☐ Document owner
☐ Document Issuer

Firearm Report

Occurrence # ______ **Badge #** ______

Classification (Select all that apply)**

☐ Commercial
☐ Counterfeit
☐ Evidence
☐ Found
☐ Fraud
☐ Held
☐ Lost
☐ Outstanding
☐ Pawned
☐ Proceeds of crime
☐ Prohibited
☐ Recovered
☐ Restricted
☐ Safekeeping
☐ Seized
☐ Stolen
☐ Used in
☐ Used as weapon
☐ Other

Verified (Select all that apply)**

☐ Source: Accused
☐ Source: Complainant
☐ Source: Witness
☐ Source: Informant
☐ Police occurrence
☐ Police street check
☐ Police custody
☐ Police records
☐ Police investigation
☐ Police CAD
☐ CPIC
☐ Birth certificate
☐ SIN card
☐ Photo ID
☐ Other ______

Make: ______ **Model:** ______ **Year:** ______

Manuf. Date: ______ **Serial#:** ______ **Aux.Serial #:** ______

Original Colours: ______ / ______ **Common name:** ______

Value (original):** ______ **Value (current):**** ______ **Registered:** ☐ **Registry check date:** ______

Caliber: ______ **Barrel:** ______ **Shots:** ______

Remarks: ______

Relate to person/business: ______ **DOB:** ______

Involvement (Select one)

☐ Driver
☐ Finder
☐ Leases
☐ Owner
☐ Passenger
☐ Renter
☐ Seized from
☐ Appraiser
☐ Document owner
☐ Document owner
☐ Document Issuer

Firearm Type & Descriptions (Select only one firearm description from this box)

Prohibited Weapon
☐

Restricted Weapon
☐ Air gun
☐ Bolt action
☐ Breech/muzzle loader
☐ Flare and tear gas
☐ Fully automatic
☐ Lever action
☐ Multi-barrel
☐ Pump action
☐ Revolver
☐ Semi-automatic
☐ Single shot

Rifle
☐ Air gun
☐ Automatic
☐ Bolt action
☐ Breech/muzzle loader
☐ Flare/tear gas
☐ Lever action
☐ Multi-barrel
☐ Other rifles
☐ Pump action
☐ Semi-automatic
☐ Single shot

Shotgun
☐ Air gun
☐ Automatic
☐ Breech/muzzle loader
☐ Flare and tear gas
☐ Fully automatic
☐ Lever action
☐ Multi-barrel
☐ Other shotguns
☐ Pump action
☐ Semi-automatic
☐ Single shot

Other guns and parts
☐ Air pistol / handgun
☐ Antique
☐ Barrel
☐ Bolt
☐ Case
☐ Clip
☐ Cylinder
☐ Fore grip
☐ Grip
☐ Magazine
☐ Paintball
☐ Receiver
☐ Sights, scope
☐ Sling, swivel
☐ Speed loader
☐ Stock

Fraudulent Document Report Occurrence # ______ Badge # ______

Occurred Date & Time: ______ to ______

Report Date & Time: ______

Remarks: ______

Victim Name: ______ **Victim Type:** ______

Report reason (Select one)

- ☐ Certificate Forged
- ☐ Endorsement forged
- ☐ Other
- ☐ No account
- ☐ Non-sufficient funds
- ☐ Signature forged
- ☐ Stolen
- ☐ Account closed
- ☐ Amount raised

Document type (Select one)

- ☐ Company cheque
- ☐ Counter cheque
- ☐ Credit card
- ☐ Government cheque
- ☐ Invoice
- ☐ Money order
- ☐ Payroll cheque
- ☐ Personal cheque
- ☐ Sales draft
- ☐ Traveller's cheque
- ☐ Other

Date of Document: ______ **Issued by:** ______

Branch: ______ **Account/Document #:** ______

Document sequence #: ______ **Payable to:** ______

Signed by: ______ **Value:** ______

Amount received: ______ **Portion written by Complainant:** ______

Portion written by suspect: ______

Identification Used

Driver's licence #: ______ **Province:** ______

Vehicle licence #: ______ **Province:** ______

Make: ______ **Model:** ______ **Colour:** ______

Card Type (Select one)

- ☐ American Express
- ☐ ATM card
- ☐ Canadian Tire
- ☐ Diner's Club
- ☐ En Route
- ☐ Esso
- ☐ Mastercard
- ☐ PetroCanada
- ☐ Sears
- ☐ Shell
- ☐ Simpson's
- ☐ Sunoco
- ☐ Texaco
- ☐ Trust Company
- ☐ Visa
- ☐ Zellers
- ☐ Other store
- ☐ Other Oil/Gas
- ☐ Other

Issued by: ______

Card #: ______ **Telephone #:** ______

Narrative on Back

Narrative ____

General Occurrence Report **Occurrence #** **Badge #**

Occurrence Date & Time: ______________________ **TO** ______________________

Reported Date & Time: ______________________

Location: ______________________ **Incident Type:** ______________________

Narrative

Continue on back

General Property Report

Occurrence # **Badge #**

Classification (Select all that apply)**

- ☐ Commercial
- ☐ Counterfeit
- ☐ Evidence
- ☐ Found
- ☐ Fraud
- ☐ Held
- ☐ Lost
- ☐ Outstanding
- ☐ Pawned
- ☐ Proceeds of crime
- ☐ Prohibited
- ☐ Recovered
- ☐ Restricted
- ☐ Safekeeping
- ☐ Seized
- ☐ Stolen
- ☐ Used in
- ☐ Used as weapon
- ☐ Other

Verified (Select all that apply)**

- ☐ Source: Accused
- ☐ Source: Complainant
- ☐ Source: Witness
- ☐ Source: Informant
- ☐ Police occurrence
- ☐ Police street check
- ☐ Police custody
- ☐ Police records
- ☐ Police investigation
- ☐ Police CAD
- ☐ CPIC
- ☐ Birth certificate
- ☐ SIN card
- ☐ Photo ID
- ☐ Other

Property #1 Type (Select one)**

- ☐ Appliance
- ☐ Computer/parts
- ☐ Consumable goods
- ☐ Household Articles
- ☐ Jewellery
- ☐ Machinery or tools
- ☐ Musical instrument
- ☐ Office equipment
- ☐ Personal accessories
- ☐ Photographic equipment
- ☐ Radio, TV, etc
- ☐ Scientific or Optical devices
- ☐ Sporting good
- ☐ Vehicle accessory
- ☐ Other article

Description: ______

Make: ______ **Model:** ______ **Year:** ______

Manufacture Date: ______ **Serial #:** ______ **Aux. Serial #:** ______

Original Colours: ______ / ______ **Common name:** ______

Original Value:** ______ **Current Value:**** ______ **Quantity:** ______

Remarks: ______

Property #2 Type (Select one)**

- ☐ Appliance
- ☐ Computer/parts
- ☐ Consumable goods
- ☐ Household Articles
- ☐ Jewellery
- ☐ Machinery or tools
- ☐ Musical instrument
- ☐ Office equipment
- ☐ Personal accessories
- ☐ Photographic equipment
- ☐ Radio, TV, etc
- ☐ Scientific or Optical devices
- ☐ Sporting good
- ☐ Vehicle accessory
- ☐ Other article

Description: ______

Make: ______ **Model:** ______ **Year:** ______

Manufacture Date: ______ **Serial #:** ______ **Aux. Serial #:** ______

Original Colours: ______ / ______ **Common name:** ______

Original Value:** ______ **Current Value:**** ______ **Quantity:** ______

Remarks: ______

Relate to person/business: ______ **DOB:** ______

Involvement (Select one)

- ☐ Driver
- ☐ Finder
- ☐ Leases
- ☐ Owner
- ☐ Passenger
- ☐ Renter
- ☐ Seized from
- ☐ Appraiser
- ☐ Document owner
- ☐ Document owner
- ☐ Document Issuer

Involved Person Report

Occurrence # ______ **Badge #** ______

***Classification** (up to 3 picks)
☐ Arrested ☐ Accused ☐ Attending Physician ☐ Charged ☐ Complainant ☐ Coroner ☐ Cyclist ☐ Deceased
☐ Escapee ☐ Finder ☐ Located ☐ Missing ☐ NOK ☐ Owner ☐ Pedestrian ☐ Reporter
☐ Suicidal ☐ Suspect ☐ Vehicle driver ☐ Vehicle passenger ☐ Victim(crime person) ☐ Victim(property crime) ☐ Victim(OMPPAC) ☐ Wanted
☐ Warned ☐ Witness ☐ YO under 16 ☐ YO 16-17 criminal offence ☐ Child under 12 ☐ Other

***Verified** (up to 3 picks)
☐ Source: Accused ☐ Source: Complainant ☐ Source: Witness ☐ Source: Informant
☐ Police occurrence ☐ Police street check ☐ Police custody ☐ Police records
☐ Police investigation ☐ Police CAD ☐ CPIC ☐ Birth certificate
☐ SIN card ☐ Photo ID ☐ Other (specify below) ______

ID FPS #: ______ Deceased (date): ______
Drivers licence #: ______ Class: ______ Province or State of Issue: ______

***Name** Surname: ______ G1 ______ G2 ______ G3 ______
Sex: ______ DOB: ______
Name Type: ☐ Primary ☐ Alias ☐ Nickname ☐ Maiden name ☐ Variant ☐ Acronym ☐ Legal ☐ Operating ☐ Other

Other Name Surname: ______ G1 ______ G2 ______
Sex: ______ DOB: ______
Name Type: ☐ Alias ☐ Nickname ☐ Maiden name ☐ Variant ☐ Acronym ☐ Legal ☐ Operating ☐ Other

***Address** Type: ☐Residence ☐Seasonal ☐Temporary ☐Business ☐NFA ☐Frequents ☐Observed ☐Other
Effective to date: ______ Include address in Crown brief? (Y/N): ______
Verified how (use above) ______
St/Fire # ______ Street: ______ Type: ______ Dir: ______
Mun./Twp: ______ Region: ______ Prov./State: ______
Postal Code: ______ Country: ______ ☐Apt ☐Suite ☐Unit: ______
Common Name: ______ Zone: ______
Phone # : (   ) ______
Rural Details: Lot #: ______ Con #: ______ Site #: ______
Mailing address details: Box: ______ Route: ______ Postal district: ______

***UCR Type**:
☐ Unknown ☐ Hotel ☐ Gas station ☐ Parking lots ☐ Other non-commercial place ☐ Other public transportation
☐ Single Home ☐ Car dealership ☐ Supervised school ☐ Street or highway
☐ Private property ☐ Financial institution ☐ Unsupervised school ☐ Open areas ☐ Other commercial place ☐ Subway or subway station
☐ Apartment ☐ Convenience store ☐ College ☐ Bus or Bus shelter

Description **Height:** ______ **Weight:** ______ **Build:** ______
Race: ______ **Hair Colour:** ______ **Eye Colour:** ______

Person Information
Birthplace: ______ Province: ______ Country: ______ Citizenship: ______
Marital Status: ______ Language: ______ Translator needed: ___ Employer: ______
Native status: ☐ Metis ☐ Non-native ☐ Non status Indian ☐ Unknown/not reported ☐ Status Indian off reserve ☐ Status Indian on reserve
Native Band: ______

Description Details

Appearance

Complexion: ☐ Dark ☐ Medium ☐ Light/Fair ☐ Albino ☐ Ruddy ☐ Sallow
Facial skin: ☐ Freckled ☐ Moles ☐ Pimples/pockmarked

Hair

Partly grey (Y/N): ______ Secondary colour: ______
Style: ☐ Afro ☐ Bushy ☐ Braided ☐ Curly ☐ Dreadlocks ☐ Mohawk ☐ Ponytail
☐ Punk ☐ Rat tail ☐ Spiked ☐ Straight ☐ Unkempt ☐ Wavy
Length: ☐ Short ☐ Medium ☐ Long ☐ Brush cut ☐ Shaved ☐ Mixed
Loss: ☐ None ☐ Bald ☐ Part bald ☐ Receding ☐ Thin
Parting: ☐ None ☐ Left ☐ Right ☐ Middle
Miscellaneous: ☐ Wig/Toupee ☐ Implants ☐ Extensions
Beard: ☐ None ☐ Unshaven ☐ Full ☐ Partial ☐ Scraggly ☐ Goatee ☐ Other
Beard Colour: ______
Moustache: ☐ None ☐ Unshaven ☐ Thin ☐ Medium ☐ Thick ☐ Fumanchu
Moustache Colour: ______
Sideburns: ☐ None ☐ Sideburns ☐ Muttonchops

Eyes

Secondary colour: ______
Lenses: ☐ Glasses ☐ Contacts ☐ Contacts-Color ☐ Monocle ☐ Sunglasses ☐ Other
Cast: ☐ None ☐ Left ☐ Right ☐ Cross-eyed
Blind: ☐ Left blind ☐ Right blind ☐ Left missing ☐ Right missing ☐ Left artificial ☐ Right artificial

Miscellaneous

Dental: ☐ Broken/missing upper ☐ All missing upper ☐ Partial dentures (upper)
☐ Full denture (upper) ☐ Broken missing/lower ☐ All missing lower
☐ Partial dentures (lower) ☐ Full dentures(lower) ☐ Silver/gold
☐ Decayed ☐ Upper protrude/overbite ☐ Lower protrude/ underbite
☐ Crooked/irregular ☐ Capped ☐ Braces
☐ Stained ☐ Stud ☐ Gaps
Ears: ☐ Cauliflower ☐ Protruding ☐ Flat ☐ Pointed ☐ Large ☐ Small
☐ Left missing ☐ Right missing ☐ Other
Handed: ☐ Right ☐ Left ☐ Ambidextrous
Speech: ☐ Accent ☐ Lisp ☐ Stutter ☐ Quiet
Miscellaneous: ☐ Effeminate ☐ Limp ☐ Deaf ☐ Mute ☐ Mental handicap
☐ Harelip ☐ Cleft palate ☐ Cleft chin ☐ Br/hump nose ☐ Heavy eyebrows
☐ Cross dresser ☐ Crutches ☐ Wheelchair ☐ Effeminate w/masculine

Marks (ONLY THE FOLLOWING TYPES MAY BE USED)

Mark Types		Tattoo Types				
Pierced	Birthmark	Animal	Cross	Grim Reaper	Mark	Other
Burn Scar	Amputation	Arrow	Devil	Heart	Nautical	
Mole	Wart	Banner, Scroll	Dragon	Indian	Snake	
Tattoo	Deformity	Bird	Emblem, Flag	Knife, Sword	Wings	
Scar		Bones, Skull	Flower	Marijuana	Woman	
		Cat, Tiger, etc	Gang	Man	Word, Name	

1) Type: ______ Location: ______ Size(in/cm): ______ Tattoo Type: ______
Description: ______
2) Type: ______ Location: ______ Size(in/cm): ______ Tattoo Type: ______
Description: ______
3) Type: ______ Location: ______ Size(in/cm): ______ Tattoo Type: ______
Description: ______
4) Type: ______ Location: ______ Size(in/cm): ______ Tattoo Type: ______
Description: ______

Clothing Descriptors

Description: ______

Missing Person Report **Occurrence #** **Badge #**

Report Date & Time: ______

Missing: ______ **DOB:** ______

Missing Type (Select one)

☐ Eloped ☐ Missing ☐ Young Offender ☐ Other ☐ Compassion to Locate

Missing between: ______ & ______

Probable Reason (Select one)

☐ Abduction by stranger
☐ Accident
☐ Parental abduction-court order
☐ Parental abduction-no court order
☐ Runaway
☐ Unknown
☐ Wandered off/lost
☐ Other

From (Select one)

☐ Child care service
☐ Detention centre
☐ Disaster
☐ Family residence
☐ Foster home
☐ School
☐ Shopping mall
☐ Vacation/travel
☐ Work/work related
☐ Youth centre
☐ Other institution
☐ Other

History (Select one)

☐ Habitual/chronic ☐ No history ☐ Repeat

Dental (Select one)

☐ Available- not entered
☐ Available- partial not entered
☐ Entered
☐ Entered partial
☐ Not required
☐ Unavailable

Photo (Select one)

☐ Available- not entered
☐ Available- partial not entered
☐ Entered
☐ Entered partial
☐ Not required
☐ Unavailable

X-Rays (Select one)

☐ Available- not entered
☐ Available- partial not entered
☐ Entered
☐ Entered partial
☐ Not required
☐ Unavailable

Disability/Dependency (Multiples allowed)

☐ Alcohol
☐ Drugs
☐ Medical
☐ Mental Disability
☐ Physical disability
☐ Solvent abuse
☐ Suicide Risk
☐ Other

Footprint Available

☐ Yes ☐ No

Circumcision

☐ Yes ☐ No

Blood Type

☐ A Positive
☐ A Negative
☐ A Unknown
☐ B Positive
☐ B Negative
☐ B Unknown
☐ O Positive
☐ O Negative
☐ O Unknown
☐ AB Positive
☐ AB Negative
☐ AB Unknown

Probable destination: ______

Institution: ______ **Order Expiry Date(s):** ______

Date last seen: ______ **By:** ______ **at** ______

Remarks: ______

Narrative on Back

Narrative ____

Notes Report **Occurrence #** **Badge #**

Task #: ______ **Reported Date & Time:** ______

Remarks: ______

Narrative

Continue on back

Police Document Report **Occurrence #** **Badge #**

Classification (Select all that apply)**

☐ Commercial
☐ Counterfeit
☐ Evidence
☐ Found
☐ Fraud
☐ Held
☐ Lost
☐ Outstanding
☐ Pawned
☐ Proceeds of crime
☐ Prohibited
☐ Recovered
☐ Restricted
☐ Safekeeping
☐ Seized
☐ Stolen
☐ Used in crime
☐ Used as weapon
☐ Other

Verified (Select all that apply)**

☐ Source: Accused
☐ Source: Complainant
☐ Source: Witness
☐ Source: Informant
☐ Police occurrence
☐ Police street check
☐ Police custody
☐ Police records
☐ Police investigation
☐ Police CAD
☐ CPIC
☐ Birth certificate
☐ SIN card
☐ Photo ID
☐ Other ____________

Police Document (Select one)**

☐ CD-ROM/floppy disk
☐ Notebook
☐ Police form
☐ Police photos
☐ PON book
☐ Tape (video)- surveillance
☐ Tape (video)- statement
☐ Tape (audio)- surveillance
☐ Tape (audio)- statement
☐ Other

Start: ____________ **End:** ____________

Common Name: ____________

Remarks: ____________

Classification (Select all that apply)**

☐ Commercial
☐ Counterfeit
☐ Evidence
☐ Found
☐ Fraud
☐ Held
☐ Lost
☐ Outstanding
☐ Pawned
☐ Proceeds of crime
☐ Prohibited
☐ Recovered
☐ Restricted
☐ Safekeeping
☐ Seized
☐ Stolen
☐ Used in crime
☐ Used as weapon
☐ Other

Verified (Select all that apply)**

☐ Source: Accused
☐ Source: Complainant
☐ Source: Witness
☐ Source: Informant
☐ Police occurrence
☐ Police street check
☐ Police custody
☐ Police records
☐ Police investigation
☐ Police CAD
☐ CPIC
☐ Birth certificate
☐ SIN card
☐ Photo ID
☐ Other ____________

Police Document (Select one)**

☐ CD-ROM/floppy disk
☐ Notebook
☐ Police form
☐ Police photos
☐ PON book
☐ Tape (video)- surveillance
☐ Tape (video)- statement
☐ Tape (audio)- surveillance
☐ Tape (audio)- statement
☐ Other

Start: ____________ **End:** ____________

Common Name: ____________

Remarks: ____________

Relate to person/business: ____________ **DOB:** ____________

Involvement (Select one)

☐ Driver
☐ Finder
☐ Leases
☐ Owner
☐ Passenger
☐ Renter
☐ Seized from
☐ Appraiser
☐ Document owner
☐ Document owner
☐ Document Issuer

Police Investigative Tool Report

Occurrence # **Badge #**

Classification (Select all that apply)**

☐ Commercial
☐ Counterfeit
☐ Evidence
☐ Found
☐ Fraud
☐ Held
☐ Lost
☐ Outstanding
☐ Pawned
☐ Proceeds of crime
☐ Prohibited
☐ Recovered
☐ Restricted
☐ Safekeeping
☐ Seized
☐ Stolen
☐ Used in crime
☐ Used as weapon
☐ Other

Verified (Select all that apply)**

☐ Source: Accused
☐ Source: Complainant
☐ Source: Witness
☐ Source: Informant
☐ Police occurrence
☐ Police street check
☐ Police custody
☐ Police records
☐ Police investigation
☐ Police CAD
☐ CPIC
☐ Birth certificate
☐ SIN card
☐ Photo ID
☐ Other ____________

Investigative Tool (Select one) **

☐ DNA
☐ Ident impression casting
☐ Latent print
☐ Sex assault kit
☐ Gunshot residue kit
☐ Other

Start: ____________ **End:** ____________

Common Name: ____________ ____________

Remarks: ____________

Classification (Select all that apply)**

☐ Commercial
☐ Counterfeit
☐ Evidence
☐ Found
☐ Fraud
☐ Held
☐ Lost
☐ Outstanding
☐ Pawned
☐ Proceeds of crime
☐ Prohibited
☐ Recovered
☐ Restricted
☐ Safekeeping
☐ Seized
☐ Stolen
☐ Used in crime
☐ Used as weapon
☐ Other

Verified (Select all that apply)**

☐ Source: Accused
☐ Source: Complainant
☐ Source: Witness
☐ Source: Informant
☐ Police occurrence
☐ Police street check
☐ Police custody
☐ Police records
☐ Police investigation
☐ Police CAD
☐ CPIC
☐ Birth certificate
☐ SIN card
☐ Photo ID
☐ Other ____________

Investigative Tool (Select one)

☐ DNA
☐ Ident impression casting
☐ Latent print
☐ Sex assault kit
☐ Gunshot residue kit
☐ Other

Start: ____________ **End:** ____________

Common Name: ____________ ____________

Remarks: ____________

Relate to person/business: ____________ **DOB:** ____________

Involvement (Select one)

☐ Driver
☐ Finder
☐ Leases
☐ Owner
☐ Passenger
☐ Renter
☐ Seized from
☐ Appraiser
☐ Document owner
☐ Document owner
☐ Document Issuer

Security Report

Occurrence # ______ **Badge #** ______

Classification (Select all that apply)**

- ☐ Commercial
- ☐ Counterfeit
- ☐ Evidence
- ☐ Found
- ☐ Fraud
- ☐ Held
- ☐ Lost
- ☐ Outstanding
- ☐ Pawned
- ☐ Proceeds of crime
- ☐ Prohibited
- ☐ Recovered
- ☐ Restricted
- ☐ Safekeeping
- ☐ Seized
- ☐ Stolen
- ☐ Used in
- ☐ Used as weapon
- ☐ Other

Verified (Select all that apply)**

- ☐ Source: Accused
- ☐ Source: Complainant
- ☐ Source: Witness
- ☐ Source: Informant
- ☐ Police occurrence
- ☐ Police street check
- ☐ Police custody
- ☐ Police records
- ☐ Police investigation
- ☐ Police CAD
- ☐ CPIC
- ☐ Birth certificate
- ☐ SIN card
- ☐ Photo ID
- ☐ Other ______

Security #1 Type (Select one)**

- ☐ Canadian currency
- ☐ U.S. currency
- ☐ Foreign currency
- ☐ Money order/travel cheque
- ☐ Other securities
- ☐ Passports
- ☐ Corporate bonds
- ☐ Credit card
- ☐ Debit card
- ☐ Government bonds
- ☐ Stocks
- ☐ Identification
- ☐ Vehicle document
- ☐ Other

Description: ______

Issued by: ______ **Common name:** ______

Name: ______, ______, ______

Serial #: ______ **Serial # range end:** ______

Sequence: ______ **Expiry date:** ______ **Value:** ______

Remarks: ______

Security #2 Type (Select one)**

- ☐ Canadian currency
- ☐ U.S. currency
- ☐ Foreign currency
- ☐ Money order/travel cheque
- ☐ Other securities
- ☐ Passports
- ☐ Corporate bonds
- ☐ Credit card
- ☐ Debit card
- ☐ Government bonds
- ☐ Stocks
- ☐ Identification
- ☐ Vehicle document
- ☐ Other

Description: ______

Issued by: ______ **Common name:** ______

Name: ______, ______, ______

Serial #: ______ **Serial # range end:** ______

Sequence: ______ **Expiry date:** ______ **Value:** ______

Remarks: ______

Relate to person/business: ______ **DOB:** ______

Involvement (Select one)

- ☐ Driver
- ☐ Finder
- ☐ Leases
- ☐ Owner
- ☐ Passenger
- ☐ Renter
- ☐ Seized from
- ☐ Appraiser
- ☐ Document owner
- ☐ Document owner
- ☐ Document Issuer

Sudden Death/Homicide Report Occurrence # Badge #

Report Date & Time: ____________________

Deceased: ____________________ DOB: ____________________

Type (Select one)

☐ Homicide ☐ Sudden death ☐ Suicide ☐ Other ☐ Unknown

Date & Time of Death from: ____________________ To ____________________

Pronounced dead by: ____________________ Telephone #: ____________________ Time: __________

Coroner/Pathologist

Coroner: ____________________ Telephone #: ____________________ Time: __________

Pathologist: ____________________ Telephone #: ____________________ Time: __________

Post Mortem Date & Time: ____________________

Next of Kin

Name: ____________________ Telephone #: ____________________

Notified by: ____________________ Date & Time: ____________________

Body

Released by: ____________________ Date & Time: ____________________

Taken by: ____________________ Date & Time: ____________________

Taken to: ____________________

Weapon: ____________________ Motive: ____________________

Cause of Death: ____________________

Identity established: ____________________

Remarks: ____________________

Narrative on back

Narrative: ______________________________

Supplementary Report Occurrence # Badge #

Reported Date & Time: ____

Remarks: ____

Narrative

Continue on back

Vehicle Report

Occurrence # ______ **Badge #** ______

Classification (Select all that apply)**

☐ Abandoned
☐ Crime
☐ Damaged
☐ Involved in Accident
☐ Found
☐ Held
☐ Lost
☐ Outstanding
☐ Recovered
☐ Released
☐ Repossessed
☐ Seized
☐ Stolen
☐ Street Check
☐ Suspect
☐ Towed
☐ Other
☐ Doors Locked
☐ Keys in Vehicle

Verified (Select all that apply)**

☐ Source: Accused
☐ Source: Complainant
☐ Source: Witness
☐ Source: Informant
☐ Police occurrence
☐ Police street check
☐ Police custody
☐ Police records
☐ Police investigation
☐ Police CAD
☐ CPIC
☐ Birth certificate
☐ SIN card
☐ Photo ID
☐ Other ______

Recovery (Select one)

☐ Not applicable
☐ Not recovered
☐ No damage
☐ Parts missing
☐ Damaged
☐ Destroyed-not burned
☐ Destroyed-burned
☐ Condition unknown

Make: ______ **Model:** ______ **Year:** ______

Manufacture Date: ______ **VIN #:** ______ **Aux. Serial #:** ______

Original Colours: ______ / ______ **Repainted Colours:** ______ / ______

Original Value:** ______ **Current Value:**** ______

Common name: ______

Licence #: ______ **Prov/state:** ______ **Tag:** ______ **Date:** ______

Plate type (Select one)

☐ Antique
☐ ATV
☐ Bus
☐ Commercial
☐ Dealer
☐ Diplomatic
☐ Farm
☐ Government
☐ Military
☐ Motorcycle
☐ Passenger
☐ Snowmobile
☐ Trailer
☐ Transit Permit
☐ **Other**

Remarks: ______

Relate to person/business: ______ **DOB:** ______

Involvement (Select one)

☐ Driver
☐ Finder
☐ Leases
☐ Owner
☐ Passenger
☐ Renter
☐ Seized from
☐ Appraiser
☐ Document owner
☐ Document owner
☐ Document Issuer

Continue on back

Vehicle Report

Vehicle Type & Descriptions (Select only one vehicle description from this box)

All terrain vehicle

☐ Amphibious vehicle
☐ ATV 3 wheel
☐ ATV 4 wheel- 2wd
☐ ATV 4 wheel- 4wd
☐ ATV 6 wheel
☐ ATV 8 wheel
☐ Dune buggy
☐ Hover craft
☐ Other

Automobile

☐ 2 door automobile
☐ 2 door convertible
☐ 2 door hatchback
☐ 3 door automobile
☐ 4 door automobile
☐ 4 door convertible
☐ 4 door hatchback
☐ Armoured car
☐ Hearse
☐ Limousine
☐ Police automobile
☐ Sedan
☐ Sports car
☐ Station wagon
☐ SUV
☐ Taxi

Bus, coach, streetcar, train

☐ Ambulance bus
☐ Bus/coach- general
☐ Double-decker bus
☐ Freight train
☐ LRT train
☐ Minibus
☐ Police bus/ coach
☐ Railroad car
☐ Passenger train
☐ School bus
☐ Subway train
☐ Trolley bus
☐ Tracked vehicle
☐ Other bus/ train

Construction equipment

☐ Backhoe
☐ Bulldozer
☐ Chain trencher
☐ Concrete mixer
☐ Construction vehicle
☐ Container dump truck
☐ Grader
☐ Forklift truck
☐ Mobile crane
☐ Skid- loader
☐ Snowplough
☐ Steam roller
☐ Other heavy vehicle

Farm Equipment

☐ Baler
☐ Combine
☐ Cultivator
☐ Garden cultivator
☐ Harrow
☐ Manure spreader
☐ Plough
☐ Swather
☐ Tiller
☐ Tractor
☐ Other farm vehicle
☐ Wagon

Motorcycle

☐ Minibike
☐ Moped
☐ Motorcycle
☐ Motor scooter
☐ Police motorcycle
☐ Sidecar
☐ Off-road motorcycle
☐ Other motorcycle

Motor Home, RV

☐ Motor home
☐ Other RV

Snowmobile

☐ Other snowmobile

Trailer

☐ Camping trailer
☐ Horse trailer
☐ House trailer
☐ Semi-trailer
☐ Snowmobile trailer
☐ Utility trailer
☐ Other trailer

Truck, Van

☐ Armoured car
☐ Armoured van
☐ Camper truck
☐ Dump truck
☐ Garbage truck
☐ Mail truck
☐ Mail van
☐ Mini van
☐ Moving van/truck
☐ Panel truck
☐ Pickup truck
☐ Police truck
☐ Police van
☐ Pumper truck
☐ Refrigerated truck
☐ Semi-tractor
☐ Stake truck
☐ Tanker truck
☐ Tow truck
☐ Other van
☐ Other truck

Other motorized

☐ Fire department vehicle

Victim's Report

Occurrence # ____ **Badge #** ____

Victim: ______________________ **DOB:** ____________

Violation against Victim (Select one)

☐ Murder 1st Degree
☐ Murder 2nd Degree
☐ Manslaughter
☐ Infanticide
☐ Criminal Negligence cause death
☐ Attempted murder
☐ Conspire to commit murder
☐ Aggravated sexual assault
☐ Sexual Assault w/weapon
☐ Sexual Assault
☐ Other sexual crimes
☐ Aggravated assault
☐ Assault weapon/ cause BH
☐ Assault Level 1
☐ Discharge firearm with intent
☐ Assault peace/public officer
☐ Criminal Negligence causing BH
☐ Other assaults
☐ Kidnapping
☐ Hostage taking
☐ Abduction under 14 yr.
☐ Abduction under 16 yr.
☐ Removal of children from Canada
☐ Abduction – custody order
☐ Abduction – no custody order
☐ Robbery
☐ Extortion
☐ Criminal Harassment
☐ Utter threats to person
☐ Explosives cause death/BH
☐ Arson-disregard human life
☐ Other violent violations
☐ Dangerous operation - death
☐ Dangerous operation - BH
☐ Dangerous operation – BH pursuit
☐ Impaired operation – death
☐ Impaired operation – BH
☐ Fail to Stop or Remain – C.C.

Violation: (select one) ☐ Attempted ☐ Completed

Weapon Causing Injury (Select one)

☐ Physical Force
☐ Rifle or Shotgun
☐ Explosives
☐ Sawed off rifle or shotgun
☐ Handgun
☐ Club
☐ Fully automatic
☐ Other piercing/cutting
☐ Unknown
☐ Knife
☐ Not applicable
☐ Other firearm
☐ Other weapon

Level of Injury (Select one)

☐ Not applicable
☐ Minor physical injury
☐ No injuries
☐ Loss of life
☐ Major physical injury
☐ Unknown

Accused is: (Select one)

☐ Unknown
☐ Spouse
☐ Seperated or Divorced
☐ Parent
☐ Child
☐ Other immediate
☐ Extended family
☐ Authority figure
☐ Boyfriend/girlfriend
☐ Ex-Boyfriend/Ex-Girlfriend
☐ Friend
☐ Business relationship
☐ Criminal relationship
☐ Casual acquaintance
☐ Stranger

Occupancy is: (Select one)

☐ Not applicable
☐ Victim & accused are residents
☐ Victim is resident
☐ Accused is resident
☐ Victim & accused are not residents
☐ Victim is resident/accused not known
☐ Victim is not resident/accused not known

Living together (Select one)

☐ Unknown ☐ Yes ☐ No

Officer status if victim (Select one)

☐ Not applicable ☐ Police ☐ Other Peace/Public officer

Watercraft Report **Occurrence #** **Badge #**

Classification (Select all that apply)**

☐ Abandoned
☐ Crime
☐ Damaged
☐ Involved in Accident
☐ Found
☐ Held
☐ Lost
☐ Outstanding
☐ Recovered
☐ Released
☐ Repossessed
☐ Seized
☐ Stolen
☐ Street Check
☐ Suspect
☐ Towed
☐ Other
☐ Doors Locked
☐ Keys in Vehicle

Verified (Select all that apply)**

☐ Source: Accused
☐ Source: Complainant
☐ Source: Witness
☐ Source: Informant
☐ Police occurrence
☐ Police street check
☐ Police custody
☐ Police records
☐ Police investigation
☐ Police CAD
☐ CPIC
☐ Birth certificate
☐ SIN card
☐ Photo ID
☐ Other

Recovery (Select one)

☐ Not applicable
☐ Not recovered
☐ No damage
☐ Parts missing
☐ Damaged
☐ Destroyed-not burned
☐ Destroyed-burned
☐ Condition unknown

Watercraft Type & Descriptions (Select only one watercraft description from this box)

Commercial/ Industrial

☐ Barge
☐ Cruise ship
☐ Ferry
☐ Fishing Boat
☐ Icebreaker
☐ Lifeboat
☐ Launch
☐ Steamship
☐ Tugboat
☐ Trawler

Houseboat ☐

Military vessel/boat ☐

Powerboat

☐ Air boat
☐ Bass boat
☐ Bow rider
☐ Cabin cruiser
☐ Car topper
☐ Racing boat
☐ Dinghy (power)
☐ Inflatable (power)
☐ Personal watercraft
☐ Ski boat
☐ Tri hull
☐ Tunnel hull
☐ V Hull
☐ Other

Police boat ☐

Sailboat

☐ Cabin
☐ Other
☐ Catamaran
☐ Day sail
☐ Racing sailboat
☐ Recreation sailboat

Other watercraft ☐

Continue on back

Watercraft Report (cont.)

Make: ______ **Model:** ______ **Year:** ______

Manuf. Date: ______ **Hull Identification Number:** ______

Original Colours: ______ / ______ **Repainted:** ______ / ______

Value (original):** ______ **Value (current):**** ______

Common name: ______

Licence #: ______ **Prov/state:** ______

Name: ______ **Registration:** ______

Port: ______

Class (Select one)

☐ Commercial/ industrial ☐ Pleasure ☐ Sport ☐ Other

Hull (Select one)

☐ Concrete
☐ Fiber (glass, kevlar)
☐ Metal
☐ Plastic
☐ Rubber
☐ Wood
☐ Other

Prop (Select one)

☐ Inboard motor
☐ Inboard/ outboard
☐ Outboard motor
☐ Sail
☐ Other

Length: ______ **Beam:** ______ **Draft:** ______

Remarks: ______

______

Relate to person/business: ______ **DOB:** ______

Involvement (Select one)

☐ Driver
☐ Finder
☐ Leases
☐ Owner
☐ Passenger
☐ Renter
☐ Seized from
☐ Appraiser
☐ Document owner
☐ Document owner
☐ Document Issuer

Additional Narrative Occurrence # Badge #

Narrative (continued)

Continue on back

Index